# Praise for Le:

Jared Wilson's new book, *Lest We Drift*, is easily the most helpful, timely, and important book I've read this year, maybe reaching back through last year as well. Always a careful expositor of the Scriptures, Jared is equally gifted as exegeting our cultural moment. If the church is prone to wander away from the gospel—and she is—Jared has given us an updated GPS reading on the direction and destination of our dangerous drift. What's my one sentence summary of my friend's new book? As soon as we start thinking of the gospel as a something instead of a Someone, it becomes a word easy to hyphenate, and Jesus becomes a Savior easy to forget.

**—Scotty Smith,** founding pastor of Christ
Community Church in Franklin, Tennessee

This sobering book is a much-needed reminder that "deconstruction," heresy, and disqualifying public sins don't ordinarily happen without warning. They typically begin with what Hebrews 2 calls "drift." I am grateful for Jared Wilson's experienced, wise counsel on these perplexing issues.

**—Thomas S. Kidd,** research professor of church
history, Midwestern Baptist Theological Seminary

As an enthusiastic participant in the gospel-centered movement and beneficiary of all Jared's books, I found this one the most direct and helpful. Jared clearly understands the dangers we face of drifting to the right or the left and calls us to the gospel, not just to a gospel-centered movement. How refreshing it is to apply the perfect life, atoning death, and victorious resurrection of Christ to the life of the church and the church leader. What a labor of love and genuine gift this book is to the larger church!

**—Clint Pressley,** president of the Southern Baptist Convention
and senior pastor at Hickory Grove Baptist Church

Jared C. Wilson provides a sobering and timely assessment of how Christians subtly—but significantly—move away from the gospel at a heart level. Wilson wisely avoids taking sides in the typical political or cultural battles that often distract us, instead choosing to focus on the deeper fears and desires that shape our attitudes and behaviors. With pastoral insight and a keen theological mind, Wilson guides us through these dangers, offering a diagnosis and a compelling case for returning to the beauty and sufficiency of Christ's good news. *Lest We Drift* is a clear and sound call to recenter our lives on the One who is our only hope—Jesus Christ.

—**Doug Logan Jr.,** president of Grimke Seminary, coauthor of *The Soul Winning Church*

Jared Wilson understands the temptations and pressures that have shaped the evangelical church. Not only does he help us understand what's happened within modern evangelicalism; he helps us understand the ways we're prone to drift. Even better, he calls us back to the beauty and power of Jesus and his gospel. Want to understand the state of the evangelical church? Read this book. Want to rivet your life and ministry on the only thing that matters? Let this book lead you past the distractions to a steadfast focus on Jesus.

—**Darryl Dash,** pastor of Grace Fellowship Church East Toronto; author of *8 Habits for Growth*

Gospel centrality in life and ministry is the Christianity of the apostles. Every generation of church leaders since New Testament times has had to fight to keep from the ever-present danger of drifting from gospel centrality into the many competing versions of the gospel that would carry us away. *Lest We Drift* is a timely reminder of the dangers of drifting, as well as a clear call to remain firmly anchored in the gospel of grace.

—**Brian Brodersen,** pastor, Calvary Chapel Costa Mesa, California

From the moment I picked it up, I couldn't put it down; *Lest We Drift* is a timely and prophetic call back to the real Jesus and real Christianity. In one sense, Jared Wilson's latest book is unique in that it maps the story of the "gospel-centered" movement over the past couple of decades—celebrating its fruitfulness while critiquing key areas where some have drifted from the message that is of "first importance" (1 Corinthians 15:3). But in another way, it is exactly what readers of Jared have come to expect of any book he writes: it is insightful, helpful, full of wit, yet most of all, unmistakably about Jesus. I needed this book, and I highly recommend it to you!

—**Adam Ramsey,** lead pastor at Liberti Church, Gold Coast, Australia, director for Acts 29 Asia Pacific, author of *Faithfully Present* and *Truth on Fire*

In this practical book, Jared C. Wilson looks under the hood of the "gospel-centered" movement, celebrating its successes while also reflecting honestly and soberly about how it has subtly been impacted by "drift." Lovers of the good news will both be reminded of the beauty of Christ and him crucified and urged to not reduce the good news to occasional cameo appearances.

—**Philip Brown,** pastor at Redeemer Church Tauranga and coauthor of *Church and State*

# Lest We Drift

# Lest We Drift

*Five Departure
Dangers from the
One True Gospel*

## JARED C. WILSON

ZONDERVAN
REFLECTIVE

ZONDERVAN REFLECTIVE

*Lest We Drift*
Copyright © 2025 by Jared C. Wilson

Published in Grand Rapids, Michigan, by Zondervan. Zondervan is a registered trademark of The Zondervan Corporation, L.L.C., a wholly owned subsidiary of HarperCollins Christian Publishing, Inc.

Requests for information should be addressed to customercare@harpercollins.com.

Zondervan titles may be purchased in bulk for educational, business, fundraising, or sales promotional use. For information, please email SpecialMarkets@Zondervan.com.

Library of Congress Cataloging-in-Publication Data

Names: Wilson, Jared C., 1975- author.
Title: Lest we drift : five departure dangers from the one true gospel / Jared C. Wilson.
Description: Grand Rapids, Michigan : Zondervan Reflective, [2025]
Identifiers: LCCN 2024030256 (print) | LCCN 2024030257 (ebook) | ISBN 9780310155768 (paperback) | ISBN 9780310155799 (audio) | ISBN 9780310155782 (ebook)
Subjects: LCSH: Bible. Gospels--Commentaries. | Evangelicalism.
Classification: LCC BS2555.3 .W56 2025 (print) | LCC BS2555.3 (ebook) | DDC 230/.04624--dc23/eng/20240906
LC record available at https://lccn.loc.gov/2024030256
LC ebook record available at https://lccn.loc.gov/2024030257

Published in association with Don Gates of the literary agency The Gates Group, www.the-gates-group.com.

*Cover design: Jonlin Creative*
*Cover image: © EcoPic/GettyImages*
*Interior design: Sara Colley*

*Printed in the United States of America*

24 25 26 27 28 LBC 5 4 3 2 1

*This book is dedicated to every
Christian out there who,
despite the countless distractions outside
and even inside the church,
has remained stubbornly fixated on
the finished work of Christ.
Rock on.*

*Therefore we must pay much closer attention to what we have heard, lest we drift away from it.*

**—Hebrews 2:1**

# Contents

# Foreword

ALMOST FIFTY YEARS AGO, I HELPED PLANT A CHURCH IN Scranton, Pennsylvania. I was bright, enthusiastic, and in over my head. I had a high level of biblical literacy and theological knowledge, but something was missing. After a few years of being beaten up and feeling beaten down, all I wanted to do was run. I could not face another Sunday sermon. I did not want to face another leadership meeting. I was done. If it hadn't been for a man in our congregation who incarnated the love of Jesus to me, my ministry story would have been very short.

Despite my gifts and knowledge, my ministry was missing something: Jesus—his righteous life, his substitutionary sacrifice, his victorious resurrection, and his royal priestly reign. My ministry missed the fact that the Bible I seemed so skilled at using was essentially his biography. He is the Bible's help. He is the Bible's hope. He is the grace of God generously given to us. He must be central in all the church is and does. My ministry was rescued by my meeting Jesus in a fresh, new, life-and-ministry-transforming way.

When I was lost in ministry and in the years that followed,

I have been confronted by some things that continue to rescue, guide, and change me.

*The battle in ministry to keep Jesus central is a battle for the heart.* My ministry will only go where my heart has already gone.

*You can't give away in ministry what you don't already have.* If Jesus isn't the central focus and hope of your life, he won't be in your ministry.

*The kingdom of self is a costume kingdom, very skilled at masquerading as the kingdom of God.* The way you put yourself in the center of your ministry is by doing ministry. This is where the deceit lies.

*Some of our most outwardly godly acts are where are deepest idolatries live.* Like glory thieves, we will take public prayer or preaching as an opportunity to aggrandize ourselves to those who listen.

*The enemy of our souls will gladly give us our theological knowledge, biblical literacy, worship gatherings, and ministry pursuits if he can woo away our hearts.* Christian ministry that lacks the constancy of Christ centeredness is one of his evil agendas.

*There is nothing so beautiful, wise, healing, transformative, powerful, glorious, and captivating as the gospel of Jesus Christ.* The narrative of the gospel is the most thrilling and amazing story that has ever been told.

*The gospel is a well of christological glory that has no bottom.* I have dipped into this well for fifty years and continue in fresh ways to be comforted, confronted, rescued, and restored.

Because of what God has confronted me with and patiently

taught me in my years of ministry, I am very thankful for Jared Wilson and for *Lest We Drift*. I have seen this drift not only in well-known and well-regarded partners in ministry, but I have seen it in myself and in the evangelical culture around me. On this side of eternity, there is a pull inside of us to replace the gospel of Jesus Christ with something else. The scary thing is that we do this without abandoning our theology or throwing away our Bibles. For this reason, I think this book is and will always be timely and important. Wilson has thought richly and deeply about gospel drift in ways that you will find practical, insightful, and convicting, as I have. He knows us well and understands all the things that pull us away from our confidence in, and commitment to, the centrality of the gospel in life and ministry.

My counsel to you is to fire your inner lawyer and read with an open heart. Read slowly and dig deeply into each chapter. There are treasures of rescuing wisdom to be found. Every Christian would benefit from reading *Lest We Drift*, but if you are in ministry, this book is a must-read for you and your ministry team—not just once, but once a year. May your love for Jesus and your commitment to keep him central deepen and grow as you read.

**Paul David Tripp**

# Introduction

IN 2021 WHEN MIKE COSPER AND *CHRISTIANITY TODAY* produced the official postmortem of the joint phenomena of Mars Hill Church in Seattle, Washington, and its founding pastor, Mark Driscoll, the podcast itself became a kind of Rorschach test for evangelical evaluation of those times. Like many listeners of a certain age (and gender and ethnicity), I have conducted my own self-evaluative appraisal of those not-quite-halcyon days of the so-called "gospel-centered movement."

What really went wrong?

Why didn't more of us see it more clearly, and sooner?

In 2006, I was a freelance writer and stay-at-home dad taking early steps back into local church ministry after a hiatus of a couple years. That interruption in ministry was not entirely voluntary. My life had been falling apart for some time. My marriage was broken. I was depressed and even suicidal. Desperate for some glimmer of hope, I recognized that the inspirational lessons I'd learned over several years serving in "seeker-sensitive" churches were proving a thin gruel. Somebody recommended to me the sermons of John Piper and, yes, Mark Driscoll.

I recognized Piper's name but had never read any of his work or heard him speak. Driscoll was unknown to me, but I was captivated by the sheer force of authority in the preaching of both men. And I was refreshed by their persistently expositional mode of preaching. Most of all, however, I heard over and over again from both of them how central the gospel was to all of life. As a church-raised Christian in my late twenties, I was understanding for the first time that the good news of Jesus was not just for unbelievers but for believers too—that it was *for me*.

Quite quickly, I underwent a significant spiritual renewal—something I have called "gospel wakefulness." A couple years later, I was asked by our longtime attractional megachurch leader to begin teaching in the young adult ministry. And so, I was sitting in a friend's living room looking down at the September issue of *Christianity Today* with Collin Hansen's intriguing cover story staring right back at me. The "young, restless, and Reformed" stream of evangelicalism—or at least that moniker—was effectively launched from this 2006 article. At the time of his article, Hansen was an associate editor at the magazine. He would later go on to help build the massively successful parachurch organization known as The Gospel Coalition.

I picked up the magazine and began to read about the surging popularity of leaders like John Piper and Mark Driscoll among younger Calvinist evangelicals. And then I realized Hansen was describing people like me. There was a whole tribe of us out there, and from my corner of suburban

Nashville, serving in an attractional context in the land of Willow Creek–style megachurches, I didn't even know it!

Those young, restless, and Reformed people became my people. Through the nascent world of blogging, I began to connect more and more with young ministry leaders who thought like me and led like me. We started listening to the same podcasts, frequenting the same websites, and attending the same conferences. We were sold out for gospel-centrality. When publishers caught on and began publishing all the "gospely" books, we bought them. A year into planting my own gospel-driven church, I began to write them.

Around this same time, to make some extra money, I began working for an old friend of mine from Houston who started his own company that provided freelance research assistants for pastors. The Docent Research Group served busy pastors who wanted to maximize their sermon preparation time by outsourcing some of the research—commentary summaries, book synopses, outline and illustration ideas, and more. From behind the curtain, I discovered that most of Docent's clients were attractional megachurch guys, while most of Docent's researchers were young, restless, and Reformed guys like me. While serving our clients to the best of our abilities, we also hoped to influence them a little bit in the direction of greater gospel-centrality.

Two of the pastors I regularly assisted are globally recognized ministry leaders with enormous platforms. I can't say I influenced them too much, but I appreciated the opportunity. And the opportunities expanded. As Docent grew, its service options added things like writing church Bible study curricula and providing editorial work for publishing projects. And that's how I ended up working for Mark Driscoll.

I probably should say that's how I ended up working for Mark Driscoll's *people*, as I never personally interacted with the man, only with his assistants. Driscoll had his own sermon research team with Docent, so I was not involved with his work on a weekly level. I served as manuscript editor on a project-by-project basis, mostly on shorter books Mars Hill produced for their own people as free church resource products.

It was exciting to help get the message out. Driscoll's ministry had been influential in my life, so I relished the chance to serve. And as a newly "gospel-centered" guy still trying to shed the baggage of my seeker church upbringing, I thoroughly enjoyed his constant digs at fluffy, superficial churches and his persistent claim that his church would be "all about Jesus."

And then I got confused. I was a regular listener to the man's preaching, and—as a preacher myself—I was an active listener, trying to learn not just from his content, but also from his style and his structure (when there was one). I began to notice a gradual distance between the text he was ostensibly preaching from and his expositional delivery. More and more, his preaching seemed to consist of stand-up-style comedy routines, long personal stories, and soapboxy rants.

At The Gospel Coalition's 2009 National Conference, I attended Driscoll's keynote session, eager to hear his preaching of 2 Timothy 2:14–26. It was an engaging talk on practical ministry, in which he divided church folks up into three categories—positives, negatives, and neutrals—and aimed to help ministry leaders know how to interact with each. But I noticed there wasn't much Bible in it. Later, I was assigned by Driscoll's team to edit his teaching manuscript into a book chapter for inclusion in the official conference book. The overarching direction I was given was to see if I could get it more in line with a biblical exposition. It was the only project I worked on for Team Driscoll where he was apparently unhappy with the results.

Over time, I began to notice other signs of a shift taking place. Pastors of attractional churches known for their pragmatic philosophy and entertainment-driven programming began to appear as contributors on The Resurgence, the resource website of Mars Hill Church and the Acts 29 church planting network. Driscoll preached alongside Robert Schuller at the Crystal Cathedral. I thought, *What is going on?*

This was all before I became aware of things going on behind the scenes at Mars Hill. I vaguely knew about the elders who were fired, a situation most of us later learned much more about. But I was clueless at the time about the internal claims of misogyny and verbal and emotional abuse. I just recognized *a drift*. He didn't blow everything up in a day. (Few of us do.) Gradually, however, bit by bit, there was less Bible, more Driscoll, less doctrine, more marketing.

After the removal of Driscoll from the Acts 29 network, the plagiarism scandals, his dismissal from Mars Hill, the collapse of Mars Hill itself, and the wider publishing of personal stories of abuse and mistreatment, I have thought about the Driscoll–Mars Hill situation more and more in the context of the rise (and fall?) of the gospel-centered movement. It seems clear from this vantage point, so far removed from the thicket of big-attendance conferences and big-figure publishing deals, that Driscoll was above all a salesman. His brand was himself; his aim was an empire. At the time, the young, restless, and Reformed tribe was the means to that end. He has since, of course, walked back most of the related doctrinal views and repudiated the Calvinism he once relied on for his unique slice of the marketing pie. He now aligns more with those who wear their megachurch aspirations nakedly.

But while the fall of Mars Hill in Seattle provided a kind of flashpoint for the young, restless, and Reformed diaspora and the splintering of the gospel-centered movement, it is certainly not the whole of it. Tracking the devolution over the last number of years, we could point to everything from the impact of the 2016 US election and the "social justice conversation" to significant leadership transitions like John Piper's 2012 retirement from Bethlehem Baptist Church in Minneapolis, Minnesota—and the ensuing difficulties of his successor, Jason Meyer—to the passings of R. C. Sproul in 2017 and Tim Keller in 2023. If the movement was on the ropes from all of these developments and more, debates and controversies related to the COVID-19 pandemic effectively finished it off as an ideological cohesion.

There is undeniably a lot of hurt left behind by the Driscoll impact on evangelicalism, but there are also a lot of parallel reappraisals. More and more leaders my age who once seemed so committed to the ministry philosophy of gospel-centrality now seem to have moved on. And they haven't all migrated to the same place. The balkanization of the young, restless, and Reformed tribe has resulted in silos and splinters, some more substantial than others. They run the gamut from social gospel–style progressivism and Christian "wokeness" to right-wing political syncretism and legalistic fundamentalism. Even among the numbers who still hold to the doctrinal claims of Reformed theology and its implications for gospel ministry, there are now a number of factions and divisions along political and cultural lines. *I thought we were "together for the gospel."* Kevin DeYoung has outlined the fracturing this way:

> [O]n the other side of Ferguson (2014), Trump (2016), MLK50 (2018), coronavirus (2020–2021), George Floyd (2020), and more Trump (2020–2021), the remarkable coming together seems to be all but torn apart. Obviously, the biggest issue is race and everything that touches race (e.g., police shootings, Critical Race Theory, Trump), but it's not just race that divides us. It is more broadly our different instincts and sensibilities, our divergent fears and suspicions, our various intellectual and cultural inclinations. Yes, there are important theological disagreements too, and these demand the best attention of our heads and hearts. But in many instances, people who can affirm the same doctrinal commitments on paper are miles apart in their posture and practice.[1]

DeYoung goes on to create a taxonomy charting four major factions (he calls them "teams") that remain the vestiges of a previously more congenial alliance. All four factions

---

1. Kevin DeYoung, "Why Reformed Evangelicalism Has Splintered: Four Approaches to Race, Politics, and Gender," *The Gospel Coalition*, March 9, 2021, https://www.thegospelcoalition.org/blogs/kevin-deyoung/why-reformed -evangelicalism-has-splintered-four-approaches-to-race-politics-and-gender/.

may share very similar theological beliefs, but it is in their reading of the times and their discerning of what is needed for these times that they differ.

As I write this, the most recent debate among Reformed talking heads on X (formerly Twitter) is the latest development in the Christian nationalism debate—the versatility of the US Constitution. A good number of evangelicals, who in 2016 were enraged over NFL players refusing to stand in salute for the National Anthem before ball games, are today arguing that the nation's founding documents are obsolete and that a good Christian dictator would be an improvement. So, what I'm saying is, even the postures and practices change, depending on the day.

Perhaps foreshadowed by the number of former Mars Hill leaders who now identify as dechurched or exvangelicals, we have also seen the burgeoning deconstruction phenomenon among younger evangelicals become a major portion of the religious market. Optimistically, we may be more recently seeing the religious nones hit a ceiling, but the market for anti-religious refugees from institutional evangelicalism still appears to be growing.

The non-gospel alternatives are now a hydra. If one wants to be culturally engaged in one's faith, the prospect quickly becomes wearying, given the sheer number of fronts. As we've seen in many cases, the lure of attractionalism is always a present danger, especially in a Western context—especially in an *American* context—where consumerism is the true native religion. But the multitude of off-ramps from gospel faithfulness is nothing new. The biblical writers warned us about them over and over.

In response to the threat of culturally religious additions to the gospel, the apostle Paul writes in Philippians 3:16, "Only let us hold true to what we have attained."

In response to the threat of entertaining wisdom and eloquent reasoning to the gospel, he writes in 1 Corinthians 2:2, "I decided to know nothing among you except Jesus Christ and him crucified."

And in response to the threat of skepticism about the ultimacy of the gospel, the author of Hebrews writes, "We must pay much closer attention to what we have heard, lest we drift away from it" (2:1).

These texts and more warn believers everywhere that drift isn't just the potential for *those* people. It is a danger to all of us. And it is a danger we face every day from a variety of angles.

Gospel-centrality really is God's way for the Christian life and church. Gospel-centrality really is biblical. But part of doggedly committing to the centrality of Christ's finished work in all things is being sober-minded—aware of our own inclinations to add to, subtract from, or otherwise attempt to enhance or augment the powerful work of the Holy Spirit through the message of grace in Christ. It's not enough to be aware of how Mark Driscoll and others drifted. It's our own drift that calls for our attention.

Chapter One

# Do Not Swerve

## *The Dangers of Drift*

*Do not swerve to the right or to the left.*
**—Proverbs 4:27**

**"THE GOSPEL-CENTERED MOVEMENT IS DEAD."**
So commented a former ministry colleague about the present state of an erstwhile grassroots reformation that enjoyed organizational enshrinement, media domination, and church adoption to become a new normal in the evangelical subculture. But its peak seemed to peak too soon. The movement—if indeed that's what it genuinely was—proved by growing disinterest to be not much more than a fad.

For this particular armchair coroner, the primary cause of death was that the influencers and authorities of gospel-centrality failed to rise to the occasion of quickly changing cultural challenges and threats to theological orthodoxy. The movement's thought leaders were assimilated into the pacifying (and compromising) swamps of "Big Eva"[1] and thus lost their reformational fire—and their reformational credibility.

If we charted the movement's genesis, we might outline it this way:

- 2005—The Gospel Coalition (TGC) is founded by D. A. Carson and Timothy Keller
- 2006—Graeme Goldsworthy's *Gospel-Centered Hermeneutics* is published
- 2006—Together for the Gospel (T4G) is founded by Mark Dever, Ligon Duncan, Albert Mohler, and C. J. Mahaney

---

1. Big Eva is the pejorative term—short for "Big Evangelicalism"—that refers to the large network of organizations, publishers, personalities, and conferences seen as gatekeepers and outsized influencers of evangelicalism as a movement.

- 2006—The Desiring God website launches
- 2006—Mark Driscoll's *Confessions of a Reformission Rev.* is published
- 2007—The Gospel Coalition website is launched
- 2007—The Acts 29 Church Planting Network (founded in 1998) launches its first church planter "boot camp"
- 2008—Collin Hansen's book *Young, Restless, Reformed* is published

If we charted its milestones of decline, the outline might look like this:

- 2012—Sovereign Grace Ministries sex abuse lawsuits begin
- 2012—John Piper retires from Bethlehem Baptist Church
- 2013—Mark Driscoll plagiarism controversy emerges
- 2014—Mark Driscoll preemptively resigns from Mars Hill Church after elders confront him on patterns of disqualifying behavior
- 2015—Mars Hill Church network officially disbands
- 2017—R. C. Sproul dies
- 2020—Former Acts 29 church leader and influencer Darrin Patrick dies
- 2022—Final T4G Conference
- 2023—Tim Keller dies

But the story of the decline of the gospel-centered movement is told not entirely in milestones, but in the cultural context surrounding them.

Perhaps the first significant inflection point was the renewal of the larger societal discourse on race and justice. As higher-profile instances of police brutality, largely focused on the African American community, dominated the media, the wider social justice conversation demanded evangelical dialogue, and it seemed universally understood that the conversation was not going well. While some who identified with the gospel-centered movement saw a perfectly natural connection between long-established evangelical social concern and the crises around them, others saw a not-so-subtle compromise of gospel fidelity, a co-opting of worldly values in response to worldly issues. With the rise of wokeness came the resurgence of liberation theology and the social gospel.

Maybe the assemblage of such varied Reformed evangelicals had made for uneasy allies all along. What they'd initially envisioned as a togetherness for the gospel began to show stress fractures lengthening and widening by the day. Lines were drawn. Statements were drafted. Suspicions proliferated on blogs and social media, in YouTube videos and conference panels, and even from pulpits and publications. Depending on which side you took, theological drift on the other side was glaringly evident.

To this fracturing was added the philosophical chaos of the 2016 election season. For some, the choices set before American voters were clear, and anyone's confusion or hesitation about the process or its options was further proof of their heterodoxy. The whole of American evangelicalism seemed to buckle inside this cultural pressure cooker, and the gospel-centered movement as we knew it began to disintegrate.

Tribal warfare had already well begun when the COVID-19 pandemic arrived in 2020, with its debates over masks and vaccines and, eventually, the questions of government mandates and local church response.

On every test, the gospel-centered movement was determined a failure. It was deemed an attractive philosophy in theory but useless in the practice of real life. Douglas Wilson, for instance, argued that the movement didn't apply the gospel to *enough*:

> The gospel, which is at the center, must be at the center of a big circle, not a teeny one. Two questions—what is the center, and *where is the circumference?*
>
> Gospel-centered sounds great, but we need to follow up with the question, "center of *what* exactly?" The answer has to be the center of all, the center of *everything*.[2]

I find this insight a little humorous given that the major critique of the movement for so long was that the gospel was being applied to *too much*. Consider James Grant writing in *First Things* in 2009:

> There is an important distinction that must be made and maintained between the gospel, the good news regarding the life and death and resurrection and ascension of Jesus Christ, the historical event never to be repeated, and the "work" of the Christian life that flows out of it. When

---

2. Douglas Wilson, "The Great Gospel-Centered Crack-Up," *Blog and Mablog*, January 9, 2023, https://dougwils.com/the-church/s16-theology/the-intelligence-of-grace.html/.

everything becomes the gospel (gospel life, gospel work, gospel parenting, gospel speech, gospel this and that, etc. . . .), then at some point, nothing is the gospel.[3]

Grant is right, and the muddling of gospel with law is an evergreen concern in the gospel-centered movement, just as it is a concern of this book.

When some evangelical tribesmen began teasing out the gospel's implications for social concerns—a very historically evangelical project, I might add—they were overwhelmed by shouts of "just preach the gospel!" by the same gang who eventually called them "pietists" when they obeyed.

The concerns shift. A good number of those on social media who urged "just preach the gospel" in response to evangelical interest in social justice and politics are not exactly following their own advice these days.

The fellow I mentioned at the beginning of the chapter who declared the movement dead has since moved on to the growing interests among many ex-gospel-centered folk: Reformed theonomy, patriarchalism, and even Christian nationalism.

He and his new compatriots now proclaim the death of gospel-centrality from their own social soapboxes and publishing silos. But they're not the only ones, for the aforementioned societal shifts, and a thousand other reverberations coinciding, have sent many out in all kinds of (and frequently opposite) directions. It's a great diaspora from what once

---

3. James Grant, "The Danger of 'Gospel-Centered' Everything," *First Things*, October 21, 2009, https://www.firstthings.com/blogs/firstthoughts/2009/10/the -danger-of-gospel-centered-everything/.

seemed a promising global unity. While some determined that gospel-centrality as a culture was too neutral (and thus too neutered) to be of any help in the real world of culture wars and moved right, many others drawing the same conclusions moved left. Some leaders of the gospel-centered movement were deemed too married to white evangelicalism to do something about the systemic injustice enshrined in our history, our institutions, and our churches. Many pastors did their (admittedly imperfect) best to navigate uncharted cultural waters according to their understanding of the Bible, but some were accused by departing church members of being "woke" and by others of being not woke *enough*.

Still others simply abandoned the aims of the movement entirely out of lost interest, moving on to other promising trends and movements.

The center, it appears, could not hold.

All persons, and therefore all movements and institutions, are flawed. Historically speaking, we know that even the evangelical movements that have lasting influences do not have lasting energies. Movements come and go. Some enjoy resurgences and renewals. But in all religious tribes and affiliations, sinful people do sinful things. Stupid people say stupid things. And unserious people go wherever the strongest winds will take them.

There were—and are—serious deficiencies in gospel-centrality as a subcultural tribe. But the claim of this book is that there isn't anything wrong with gospel-centrality in principle or in substance. Indeed, I will argue that when we fail to see the relevance or the pertinence of gospel-centrality for literally anything we face, the failure is not with *it*, but with us.

## "Lest We Drift"

Theological drift is always a danger within evangelicalism. When Reformed evangelicals are not drawing their polemical passion from the rise of Protestantism beginning in the early sixteenth century, they are inspired by the cautionary guidance of more recent historical episodes like the Downgrade Controversy in the late 1800s of Victorian England, the Fundamentalist/Modernist controversy of the 1920s–1930s, the Southern Baptist Convention's "conservative resurgence" in response to liberalizing influences in the denomination in the late 1970s–1980s, and the concerns in the mid-1990s over Evangelicals and Catholics Together. If the early history of Christianity was fraught with the codification of orthodoxy, late Christianity has been about the enforcing of it.

We are well acquainted with the danger of drift; we seem less acquainted with our own susceptibility to it. And while we are accustomed to noticing the drift of others, we are woefully blind about noticing it among ourselves.

While the bulk of this book is concerned with the kinds of drift threatening our fidelity to the gospel—and our unity around it—it is important to establish first (and reestablish throughout) how such drift occurs. And this is the implicit claim of gospel-centrality as an ideology: that the moment we take our eyes off the center is when we begin to move away from it.

After expounding the wonders of Christ's glory in the gospel (and the prophetic freight with which it culminates), the author of Hebrews warns us, "Therefore we must pay much closer attention to what we have heard, lest we drift away from it" (2:1). One primary implication is clear: Drift from the gospel is possible, and it happens when we stop paying *ever-closer* attention to it.

And since we are people constantly distracted by a million things inside and outside of ourselves, the potential for drift is constant in our lives. Every movement, no matter how faithful, remains vulnerable, and we fool ourselves if we think we're the first to finally exorcize our institutions and organizations of this temptation. The shifts are subtler than we usually realize, but they have widespread ramifications.

D. A. Carson remarks thusly on the generational impact of drift:

> I have heard a Mennonite leader assess his own movement in this way. One generation of Mennonites cherished the gospel and believed that the entailment of the gospel lay in certain social and political commitments. The next generation assumed the gospel and emphasized the social and political commitments. The present generation identifies itself with the social and political commitments, while the gospel is variously confessed or disowned; it no longer lies at the heart of the belief system of some who call themselves Mennonites.
>
> Whether or not this is a fair reading of the Mennonites, it is certainly a salutary warning for evangelicals at large.[4]

It absolutely is.

---

4. D. A. Carson, *The Cross and Christian Ministry: Leadership Lessons from 1 Corinthians* (Grand Rapids: Baker, 2004), 63.

I have sensed a parallel phenomenon in the generational succession of the gospel-centered movement as well. With the increased speed of information transfer, the full descent of the internet age, and the reality of globalization, what once might have taken generations can now transpire in the span of a few decades. For a great many of us who came of age at the height of the seeker-sensitive church movement—initially influenced by and trained in ministry to emulate pastors like Rick Warren, Bill Hybels, and Andy Stanley—the rediscovery of Reformed theology provided a canvas upon which to work out our growing angst with the attractional ministry paradigm. In the beginning, younger Boomers and older Gen Xers set about cherishing—or at least enjoying the newness of—gospel-centrality, especially in reaction to what we were rebelling against. From this interest arose the young, restless, and Reformed phenomenon, but in just ten short years, what was new to us had become the established norm for the next generation.

Many younger Gen Xers and Millennials effectively grew up with the gospel-centered movement as the wallpaper of their church experience. This was the generation of "assumption," for which the implications proved more interesting than the gospel itself. It didn't help that many of the "cherishers" pastoring and influencing them turned out merely to be dabblers.

The watchword of the Reformation was *semper reformanda*—"always reforming"—which for its originators meant always returning to the gospel of grace, always and ever conforming to the centrality of Christ. In the spirit of Luther's first thesis, the whole life of the Christian is to be one of constant repenting, which means constantly turning *from sin* and constantly turning *to Christ*.

Gospel-centrality, in other words, is not something you can set to autopilot.

This is true even if your doctrinal fidelity is to the true gospel! The true gospel may be de-centered, placed in the lockbox of our theological basement, or simply hung on the wall of the church website. Accordingly, it provides the background for all manner of functional, ministerial, and cultural drift. For instance, nearly every mainline church where Christ and his gospel are not preached biblically or with conviction claims to affirm the historic creeds. And nearly every conservative church where political rants and legalistic tirades dominate the pulpit maintains an orthodox statement of faith in their church documents.

Drift does not usually begin at the places of doctrines and documents but at the places of discourse and disposition.

Tim Keller writes:

> Both the Bible and church history show us that it is possible to hold all the correct individual biblical doctrines and yet functionally lose our grasp on the gospel. D. Martyn Lloyd-Jones argues that while we obviously lose the gospel if we fall into heterodoxy, we can also operationally stop preaching and using the gospel on ourselves through dead orthodoxy or through doctrinal imbalances of emphasis. Sinclair Ferguson argues that there are many forms of both legalism and antinomianism, some of which are based on overt heresy but more often on matters of emphasis and spirit. It is critical, therefore, in every new generation and setting to

find ways to *communicate the gospel clearly and strikingly, distinguishing it from its opposites and counterfeits.*[5]

We will examine some of these alternate emphases in subsequent chapters, but as the urban legend tells us, the best way to spot counterfeits is to become familiar with the real thing. Since part of our tendency toward gospel drift is in fact a pervasive gospel confusion, it behooves us to establish and constantly refamiliarize ourselves with the true gospel *and* the substance of what is meant by "gospel-centrality."

## The Gospel as Center

In my arsenal of anecdotal evidence that we have entered the assumption era of evangelicalism's grasp of the good news is my experience at the start of every semester at Midwestern Baptist Theological Seminary. On the first day of my Introduction to Pastoral Ministry course, I ask the class, "What does gospel-centered mean?"

The responses begin with a sea of ponderous young faces, eyes flitting to the ceiling, lips pursed, as the question itself is run through potentials of articulation. Often a brave soul will break the ice by saying, "It means that everything should be centered on the gospel," which is an answer correct insofar as it is redundant. Yes, gospel-centered means centering on the gospel; thank you. But what does it *mean*?

For many heirs of the gospel-centered movement, being

---

5. Timothy Keller, *Center Church: Doing Balanced, Gospel-Centered Ministry in Your City* (Grand Rapids: Zondervan, 2012), 21.

gospel-centered means reading certain authors and books, visiting certain websites, attending certain conferences, and listening to certain podcasts. It may also mean using certain phraseology in one's church vision and mission statements or other slogans and jargon. It shows itself in the abundant adjectivizing and hyphenating of the word *gospel*, a trick of the trade for which I have developed a penchant bordering on cliché. (Six of my twenty-seven books include the word *gospel* in the title, including two gospel-drivens and one gospel-shaped.) *Gospel-centered* has become a buzzword, a marketing term, and a tribal identifier. At our churches, we enjoy gospel community in our gospel groups where we have gospel conversations over gospel nachos about gospel issues.

Okay. But what does it *mean*?

One of my Midwestern Seminary colleagues, the historian Thomas Kidd, notes,

> One of the first uses of anything like "gospel-centered" appeared at the end of the 19th century, in an 1899 sermon by the evangelical Congregationalist minister J. D. Jones of Bournemouth, England. Jones was reflecting on the missionary movement and the challenge posed by other world religions. Setting out the apostles' teaching as the church's authoritative guide, he proclaimed that the disciples traveled through the Mediterranean world preaching Christ crucified: "They went to preach a Gospel and their Gospel centered on the cross."[6]

---

6. Thomas Kidd, "Why Do We Say 'Gospel-Centered'?" *The Gospel Coalition*, April 21, 2021, https://www.thegospelcoalition.org/article/why-say-gospel-centered/.

Kidd goes on to note that the first uses of the term as an adjective appear in the 1960s. For some, the fact that the phrase "gospel-centered" is relatively new, historically speaking, is enough to jettison the idea altogether.

Regardless of the term's modernity, however, gospel-centrality as a concept is essentially a summation of historic Reformed theology and Protestant spirituality that adherents would argue are as old as the Bible. Seeing as the Reformation was not an innovation but rather a recovery and renewal movement, the best intentions of the latest gospel-centered initiative are not about reinvention but about recovery and renewal. That sounds idealistic, but in its paradigmatic sense, gospel-centrality is shorthand for a Reformed understanding of biblical spirituality, bringing with it distinct truth claims that give the ideology substantial implications for life and ministry.

But before we examine those truth claims, we need to be clear on the center of gospel-centrality, which is the message of the gospel itself.

As it happens, I believe we find this clarity—alongside the truth claims of gospel-centrality—in a rather important text for the discussion: 1 Corinthians 15:1–4. The apostle Paul writes,

> Now I would remind you, brothers, of the gospel I preached to you, which you received, in which you stand, and by which you are being saved, if you hold fast to the word I preached to you—unless you believed in vain.
>
> For I delivered to you as of first importance what I also received: that Christ died for our sins in accordance

with the Scriptures, that he was buried, that he was raised
on the third day in accordance with the Scriptures.

Paul proceeds from this point to reference the numerous
eyewitnesses to Christ's resurrection and to expound upon
the staggering implications of this resurrection, but in these
first four verses of the chapter we find a wealth of information
belied by their brevity. The very first thing we ought to see is
his own direct definition of the gospel. In short: Christ died
for our sins and was raised on the third day.

We could say a whole lot more about the gospel—and
in fact, the apostle Paul and the rest of the New Testament
writers do—but I would dare to say we could not say less if
we mean to state the actual good news.

This is an important consideration in the ongoing conversations about gospel issues and definitions. Just today on
social media I encountered another entry in the occasional
rhetorical exercise of defining the gospel in one's own words.
In this version, the author asked how one might share the
gospel in seven words and quoted a rather prominent church
leader's entry about God drawing near. It was a true statement, to be sure, and a thoroughly biblical one. But it mentioned nothing of the how. It lacked the specificity of what
God actually has done. Whenever we try to say in our words
what God has said perfectly well in his own, we are likely
placing our pithiness over his power.

Any articulation of the gospel that lacks the announcement of the cross and resurrection falls short of the scandal-
ous glory perfectly given to us.

To be clear, this does not mean that every sharing of the

gospel must contain the same emphases or draw out the same proportions; still less does it mean that every sharing must use the exact same words, as if the gospel is a kind of magic formula or spell. The Bible itself in its considerable commentary on and exposition of the gospel highlights multiple facets of the cross and resurrection, sometimes speaking much more about one than the other. But even the apostolic shorthand of "the cross" (as in 1 Corinthians 1:18 or Galatians 6:14) brings with it some articulation of the living, reigning Christ.

First Corinthians 15:1–4 has become a primary reference point for my own teaching on gospel-centrality, in part because Paul is so clear on what the gospel message is. Christ died for our sins and rose again. If I had to put this message in a very few of my own words, drawing from the rest of the biblical counsel on the matter, I would say that the gospel is the announcement that God saves sinners through the life, death, and resurrection of Jesus. Alternatively, I have often expressed the news like this in my preaching: Jesus died on the cross to forgive our sins and rose from the grave to secure our eternal life.

Again, we can and should say much more about these elements, but this is the irreducible complexity of the good news.

We should also note that the good news is exactly that: *news*. It is not an announcement about anything we have done or should do. It is not, didactically speaking, a word of law. The gospel is a word of pure grace. As Keller notes, "The gospel is not about what we do but about what has been done for us."[7]

The insertion of our necessary response to the news *into*

---

7. Keller, *Center Church*, 30.

the news constitutes a conflation of the gospel with its implications, a muddling of gospel and law. Such conflations are epidemic in today's discussions on the Christian life. Every time someone says complementarianism in marriage or social justice of any kind *is* the gospel, they are conflating the news with its implications. And as we have already been warned by Dr. Carson, this failure to distinguish is an early sign of drift.

Now that we've established clarity on the gospel message itself, we can take a closer look at the reasons for its centrality, especially since Paul tells us in the passage at hand that this message is "of first importance." We should not take him to mean merely initial importance or only primary importance, but *central* importance. The biblical truth claims of gospel-centrality, as derived from the text, tell us why.

1. The whole Bible is about Jesus.
2. People change by grace, not law.
3. Our ultimate validation is found not in our performance, but in Christ's.

These three claims provide the substance of gospel-centrality. If anyone asks, "What does it mean to be gospel-centered?" these are the things we should say in our response. Now, lest we drift, let's pay closer attention to each claim.

## The Gospel as Center of the Story

The whole Bible is about Jesus.

When Paul tells the Corinthian church that Christ's

dying for their sins and Christ's rising on the third day are "in accordance with the Scriptures," he is telling them that the gospel is not some divine improvisation or theological plot twist, but rather it is the culmination of all the history, prophecy, and poetry that had come before. Considered from our vantage point in history, Paul is telling us that the Old Testament is about Jesus.

Jesus himself tells us this. "You search the Scriptures because you think that in them you have eternal life; and it is they that bear witness about me" (John 5:39). Everywhere he goes, the Lord is framing his hearers' understanding of the old covenant around himself. For instance, in Luke 4, he is in the temple reading from the Isaiac scroll and declares, "Today this Scripture has been fulfilled in your hearing" (v. 21).

The apostles' preaching was almost entirely centered on the announcement of Christ and his work as the fulfillment of the Old Testament. In perhaps the very first Christian sermon, Peter's evangelistic proclamation at Pentecost, we see Christ preached from Joel and the Psalms. Preaching like this isn't just a circumstantial technique; it is demonstrating a hermeneutic. The book of Hebrews doesn't just give us isolated points at which Christ is the fulfillment of the old covenant types and shadows; it is demonstrating a hermeneutic. The New Testament tells us over and over again that the *telos* of the Bible is Jesus.

The earliest remaining extrabiblical account of early church proclamation is Irenaeus of Lyons's *On the Apostolic Preaching*, which from its second-century perspective gives us a vivid window into how early Christians would have heard the exposition of God's Word. It is wholly and intensely christological. From Old Testament to New, Irenaeus details the hermeneutic of the apostles, which is relentlessly framed around the gospel of Jesus.

Given the recent resurgence of interest in the field of biblical theology, as well as recent efforts in theological "retrieval," one may think these claims fairly obvious or uncontroversial. But I would argue that the vast majority of evangelical preaching today—not to mention the steady production of biblical content generated online and by Christian publishing houses—regularly and stubbornly misses this "first importance."

I was once speaking at a Bible conference in Southern California, presenting on Peter's Pentecost sermon and attempting to make the case for gospel-centered preaching. I made the claim that sermons that do not connect the text at hand to Christ can hardly be considered Christian sermons, even if they are preached by Christians to Christians in a Christian church setting. A concerned pastor took me aside during the break to argue against the point with me. "Unless we have a direct reference in the New Testament to the Old Testament passage at hand," he said, "we cannot preach Christ from that text." This pastor was a seasoned veteran of expository preaching, raised in and working from an evangelical tradition that prides itself on verse-by-verse preaching, one that functionally and ideologically denies the *sensus plenior*, or fuller sense, of Scripture.

His criticism reminded me of the old Spurgeon story about the young preacher insisting that we aren't to go preaching Christ always, but only when he's explicitly in the text. In a gentler tone than Spurgeon's proposed riposte,

I suggested that every text has a road to the great metropolis of the Scriptures, Christ himself, and that the job of the preacher is to find that road.

The encounter reinforced for me that Christ-centered preaching is still controversial even among sincere Christians. But to embrace Christ as the whole point of Christianity is surely to embrace him as the center of the Word his Spirit has breathed out! Certainly the early church fathers stepped into some fanciful interpretations in their employment of their hermeneutic. (For instance, the impulse of some to interpret every Old Testament appearance of a staff or a stick as a reference to the cross.) It is possible to treat the biblical text like some kind of secret code or puzzle. Spurgeon himself cautioned against inappropriate ways of spiritualizing the text in his *Lectures to My Students*. But if we do not embrace the pursuit of Jesus as the center, climax, and culmination of the entirety of the Scriptures, we run the worse risks (in my estimation) of turning the faith into mere inspiration or intellectualism. And neither inspiration nor intellectualism saves.

To center the gospel in our hermeneutics does not require us to abandon the other kinds of mental and spiritual sharpening available to us by the Spirit in the Word. Still less does it negate Christ as moral exemplar or negate the imperative teaching of the Scriptures altogether. But it puts these blessings in proper orbit around the sun of righteousness, our glorious Christ, who alone is our hope and salvation. The historical-grammatical method is an excellent exegetical tool, but it is at best a primary or intermediate step to a full and sanctifying understanding of the Bible.

Gospel-centrality, then, envisions Jesus in his rightful place: as the *telos* of the Scriptures and, thus, as the point of the whole storyline of our lives!

## The Gospel as Center of Sanctification

People change by grace, not law.

If suggesting that Jesus is the point of the whole Bible is controversial, this claim is even more so. At least, it would appear so given the way Christians overwhelmingly approach the prospect of change.

I was reminded of the cruciality of the law/gospel distinction as it applies to the work of sanctification recently when I made a tongue-in-cheek comment about a social media post from conservative political pundit Ben Shapiro.[8] Shapiro, who is Jewish, wrote, "The commandments are a pathway that draws us closer to God." I called the idea legalism, as that is precisely what a Christless focus on the law as the path to God is. But numerous evangelicals took me to the virtual woodshed, some "reminding" me of the importance of works in the Christian life, others flat-out calling me antinomian.

If we *mis*place the place of works in our understanding of Christianity, we compromise the integrity of the gospel. Christianity is unabashedly about transformation. It is not

---

8. Jared C. Wilson (@jaredcwilson), "That's legalism, Patrick," X post, April 26, 2024, https://x.com/jaredcwilson/status/1784001608872796657/.

primarily about enhancement or enlightenment. It is not about receiving a leg up or a handout. It is not about self-help or self-esteem. Christianity is about dead things becoming alive, which is not something you can achieve with a set of instructions. You need power from on high. You need something *super*natural.

To become a follower of Jesus, one must be "born again" (John 3:3), receive divine revelation (Matt. 16:17), and receive a divine epiphany (Titus 2:11) that results in resurrection (Eph. 2:5).

It is fascinating, then, that so many Christians believe the power to become a Christian is totally of grace but becoming more Christlike after the fact is powered by the law. Paul asks, "Having begun by the Spirit, are you now being perfected by the flesh?" (Gal. 3:3), and we answer, "Yes."

In our central text for gospel-centrality, he reveals more incredible depths to the good news. Paul says in 1 Corinthians 15:1 that we received this gospel, past tense. Most of us can understand that as a reference to the conversion experience. There was a moment we didn't believe the gospel, and then there was a moment we did. We passed from death to life. We have a hundred different ways of describing this: getting saved, getting rescued, becoming justified, asking Jesus into our heart, and more. But it's what Paul says next that is so crucial to our consideration of gospel-centrality. Because the good news isn't simply an entryway into the life of Christ; it is the entire mansion.

Paul uses the phrase "in which you stand" (present tense) in verse 1, and then in verse 2 he says it's by the gospel that we are "being saved" (present-future tense). We'll look at the present tense of the gospel shortly, but first we will consider the "being saved" aspect of the gospel.

I do not take the apostle here to mean there is some sense in which our salvation is lacking at conversion. There is no Justification 1.0 dependent upon some gradual upgrade. At the moment of our conversion (if we truly are converted!) we are totally justified, eternally saved, and clothed fully in the righteousness of Christ. Therefore, I believe Paul is referring to the Spirit's work of progressive sanctification in the Christian's life. We are, over time, being convicted of our sin, growing in our understanding of God and his Word, bearing fruit in keeping with repentance, pursuing holiness, and becoming more and more conformed to the image of our Savior. These experiences can be summed up in the work of sanctification. And Paul is saying this sanctification comes *by the gospel*.

Somehow, the news that the work of salvation *is done* empowers believers to work. Except, it's not "somehow." It is by the Spirit.

After 1 Corinthians 15:1–4, the next place to which I take students for the consideration of gospel-centrality is 2 Corinthians 3. In that chapter, Paul outlines the crucial contrast between law and gospel. The law/gospel dynamic presented there is in play throughout the Scriptures, actually, and is a historical hallmark of Reformed theology. It's astounding that too few evangelicals can keep the dynamic rightly situated in their understanding of Christian spirituality.

In 2 Corinthians 3, Paul affirms not just the goodness of the law, but its gloriousness as well. Contrary to those who distort gospel-centrality into modern variations of the antinomian heresy, the law does not simply exist to reveal our badness. When God tells us in his Word to do something or to be something, he really means for us to do it or be it. Thus, gospel-centrality is not gospel-*only-ism*.

But it's also very clear that while the law is good, it's only good for what it's designed to do. It can tell us what to do, but it can't give us the power to do it. Therefore, Paul says that as glorious as the law is, the gospel "surpasses it" (2 Cor. 3:10). And in verse 18, the apostle specifies how people change in a rather startling way. He says it is by beholding the glory of Christ that we are transformed into the likeness of Christ.

We think we know how people change. We *tell* them. We tell them more than once. We raise the volume. We introduce incentives to change and consequences when change doesn't take place. We give practical advice and application. But the Bible says the way people change—at least deep down, at the heart level from which all true behavioral change comes—is by the Holy Spirit working through the good news of Jesus.

Paul reiterates the supernaturality of sanctification in Titus 2:11–12, when he says it's the transforming appearance of grace that trains us to live godly lives. In Philippians 2:12–13, he says we work out our salvation only by the working *in* of God.

The implication is as evident as it is revolutionary: The extent to which you want to see people become more like Jesus is the extent to which you will center on the gospel.

In his beautiful exposition of this subject, Scottish Presbyterian pastor Thomas Chalmers writes, "Thus it is that the freer the gospel, the more sanctifying is the gospel; and the more it is received as a doctrine of grace, the more it will be felt as a doctrine according to godliness."[9] He adds:

> Salvation by grace—salvation by free grace—salvation not of works, but according to the mercy of God—salvation on such footing is not more indispensable to the deliverance of our persons from the hand of justice than it is to the deliverance of our hearts from the chill and the weight of ungodliness. Retain a single shred or fragment of legality with the gospel and we raise a topic of distrust between man and God. We take away from the power of the gospel to melt and to conciliate. For this purpose, the freer it is, the better it is.[10]

Compare this understanding of how people change not just to the way evangelicals preach and teach but also to the way we interact socially and on social media and to the way we regard our enemies or just other believers we disagree with. Is there any indication at all that, by and large, evangelicals affirm the gospel-centered approach to change? We barely evangelize as it is. We are too busy arguing, mocking, insulting, and scoffing. The idea that holding up the glory of the good news would in any way change others seems as foreign a concept to evangelicalism as it did to the pagans of Jesus' day.

---

9. Thomas Chalmers, *The Expulsive Power of a New Affection*, Crossway Short Classics (Wheaton, IL: Crossway, 2020), 65.
10. Chalmers, *Expulsive Power*, 67.

## The Gospel as Center of the Self

Our ultimate validation is found not in our performance, but in Christ's.

First Corinthians 15:1's "in which you stand" positions the Christian in the gospel in the present tense. The news wasn't just good at the moment of our conversion. It is good now. It will be good every day. We do not outgrow it, outpace it, or outlast it. The gospel is not something we should ever move on from, because, spiritually speaking, it is not something we ever *will* move on from.

The doctrinal idea most pertinent here is that of imputation—that is, in the gospel, Christ takes on our sin (as if it was his own), and we take on his righteousness (as if it was our own). Sometimes referred to as "the great exchange," the concept is one of unprecedented reversal: "For our sake he made him to be sin who knew no sin, so that in him we might become the righteousness of God" (2 Cor. 5:21). From the point of conversion, the Christian is always clothed in the righteousness of God. Thus, our ultimate validation is based not on our performance, but upon Christ's performance on our behalf.

I frame this tenet of gospel-centrality in terms of "validation" for a couple of reasons. The idea in play here is certainly justification, but using that term often leads people to think solely in terms of conversion. The doctrine of justification *sola gratia* and *sola fide* is the heart of this, but most people, I'm convinced, think of their daily lives more in terms of approval. Christians in particular are prone to thinking of these things from the framework of spiritual activity, good works, and personal devotion. In other words, their sense of God's approval or their own sense of okay-ness—their validation—derives from how they're performing religiously. "If I've been good enough, God will love me more."

I certainly felt that way for a very long part of my Christian life. My sense of validation was bound up in reading the right books, listening to the right preachers, going to church a lot, and succeeding as a Christian leader. Those are all good things, but as part of a quest for validation, I discovered I was running toward a finish line that never got closer.

This may be obvious on a personal level, but it becomes less so on the level of church programming and spiritual resourcing. For instance, when our preaching and teaching focus predominantly on obedience, inspiration, and application—with the gospel in the shadows or brought out only for a brief formulaic cameo—we implicitly reinforce the idea that spiritual performance is the grounds of our validation.

The gospel, on the other hand, tells us no amount of good works will make God love us more and no amount of sin will make God love us less. Through his work on the cross, he forever canceled the record of debt against us, and because of the imputation of Christ's righteousness—indeed, because of our spiritual union with Christ—we enjoy ultimate validation at all times, now and forever.

## How Drift Begins

The antidote to both antinomian and legalistic drifts from the gospel is knowing that people change by grace, not by law, and knowing that our ultimate validation is found not in our performance, but in Christ's. If I know grace actually changes me, I do not need to fear the law's demands. If I know grace actually empowers me, I do not need to fear the law's commands. If I know Christ's performance is my ultimate validation, I don't need to find justification (or despair) in my efforts to obey God.

When we center on the gospel—in substance, not simply in theory—we position ourselves for power, transformation, joy, and the magnification of Christ himself. But when we neglect the substance of gospel-centrality, all manner of drift can take place.

If we take our eyes off Christ as the center of the scriptural story, the Bible will become a resource only of utility, its various messages wielded or ignored because of their perceived degree of usefulness. When we fail to properly distinguish between law and gospel, whether conflating them or distorting their biblical proportions, our religion too easily becomes religiosity, and our Christianity loses its unique and powerful flavor. Finding our validation in our own performance rather than Christ's will set us adrift into all kinds of self-salvation projects, pragmatism, and consumerism.

Centering on the gospel anchors us.

The author of Hebrews does not affirm a graduation from the gospel. In fact, Hebrews 2:1 tells us to pay closer attention to the proclamation of the message presented in Hebrews 1, lest we drift away from it. Even in Hebrews 6:1, where we find the exhortation to "leave the elementary doctrine of Christ," it seems clear the "elementary doctrine of Christ" is a commitment to the old covenant rather than moving on to dwell in their culmination in him.

Commenting on this warning, Thomas Schreiner writes, "The word translated 'drift away' (παραρρυῶμεν) is used to describe 'a ring slipping off a finger.' Perhaps there is a nautical metaphor here so that we picture a ship not anchored slowly drifting out to sea."[11] What I find fascinating about this image is that neglecting the anchor or other proper securing measures is not always about forgetfulness or other accidental neglect. Sometimes a ship will drift out to sea because of one's carelessness. But sometimes a sailor may decide all the ropes don't need to be tied, that half-secure is secure enough. Believe it or not, sometimes a person may look at the anchor and decide it won't get the job done. Or, turning to Schreiner's other metaphor, it is as if they look at the rigging on the dock and decide it won't hold the boat securely. Maybe they think they know a better way. Echoing Yeats's poetic line, they decide "the centre cannot hold."[12]

More often than not in evangelicalism, this is how drift from the gospel begins—not with an outright forgetfulness of the gospel but with a functional denial of its sufficiency. In a variety of ways, we determine it isn't strong or resilient enough to get the job done. We know what works, and the gospel isn't it.

But if we are going to recover the strength of God's grace for the entirety of our lives, we must consider the array of temptations we face to doubt its sufficiency. In the face of these various lures, only the surety of the gospel will do.

---

11. Thomas R. Schreiner, *Hebrews*, Evangelical Biblical Theology Commentary (Bellingham, WA: Lexham Press, 2020), 79.

12. William Butler Yeats, "The Second Coming," in *Yeats's Poems*, ed. A. Norman Jettares (London: Macmillan, 1996), 294.

Chapter Two

# Swept along by Winds

## The Landscape of Drift

*We have this as a sure and
steadfast anchor of the soul.*
**—Hebrews 6:19**

A YOUNG MAN HAS JUST ENTERED HIS FIRST MINISTERIAL position, becoming the twenty-second senior pastor of a historic church in a midsize Southern town. He is well versed in the principles of gospel-centrality, a theological paradigm he didn't learn in seminary, but rather from his favorite authors and preachers. He looks forward to leading, God willing, a revitalization effort at a church whose members are hopeful after a long period of decline.

His first order of business is preaching expository sermons each week that culminate in Christ, beginning with Paul's letter to the Galatians. The congregation enjoys them. He is young, and his sermons are lively, if a bit long.

A few months into his pastorate, he suggests overhauling the Sunday school structure. Perhaps age-based classes aren't the best idea, given that 80 percent of the congregation is fifty-plus years old. Identifying a few capable Bible teachers, he wants to move to a seminar model, a more topical approach that will give congregants (and potential visitors) more options and facilitate intergenerational rapport. The proposal goes over like a load of bricks and becomes the first crack in the veneer of his favor with the church.

As the young pastor encounters resistance to undoing long-held programming, perceived missteps typically overlooked in the grace of the honeymoon period become more and more the subjects of deacons' meetings, hallway conversations, emails, and anonymous notes.

Deacon so-and-so, for instance, cannot understand how the young pastor can purport to preach gospel-centered sermons yet discontinue the church's customary practice of issuing an altar call. "How can you say it's a gospel sermon if there's no altar call?" he wants to know.

The honeymoon is over.

Most members endure the changes inflicted upon them, but one particular group of older saints refuses to adjust to the new Sunday school structure and begins their own class, which runs independent of the official church programming. The pastor is weary of all the resistance. Hesitant to enter into an all-out conflict with influential members of the church—who, he's been well informed, donate generously to the church funds—he suffers meekly the passive-aggressive maintenance of the status quo.

One Monday afternoon, he sits forlornly in his office and scans the gospely books on his shelves. From them he learned all about Christocentric teaching, law/gospel dynamic, and the importance of the gospel for "all of life," but now he finds them inadequate for navigating ministry *as it really is*.

*Gospel-centrality works wonderfully in the hypothetical,* he thinks, *but I might lose my job. I just moved my family across three states for this position, and within one year, I'm thinking I've made a huge mistake.*

Whatever gospel-centrality is or can be, it must say something to this situation and others like it. It must rise to the occasion of the nitty-gritty, rubber-meets-the-road of real life and ministry.

Another pastor is in a similar predicament. This fellow is middle-aged and a two-decade veteran of church leadership now pastoring in a large church setting, but he finds the regular challenges and pacing of ministry putting constant pressure on his understanding of what it means to be gospel-centered. Once young, restless, and Reformed, he has gradually succumbed to the daily onslaught of interoffice emails, budgetary concerns, and expectations of "what's next?" to the point that ministry seems bigger and more immediate than well-intentioned theological systems can handle.

Writ large, these two scenarios represent key tension points for the application of gospel-centrality. Moving from the principle to the practice is (moderately) easy to think about and write about, but it's not easy to *actually do*. Which is why, I suspect, so many once-eager adherents of gospel-centered principles have become gospel-uncentered in person.

The ordinariness of life and ministry dulls our senses to the spiritual vitality of the good news, and thus its supernatural import for, yes, *all things*. The routine of ministry sedates us to the point where we begin to treat the gospel as routine. The effect is that even when "big" ministerial or cultural challenges arise, we do not immediately turn to the gospel as sufficient for the circumstances. It seems now so thin, so fragile.

I propose that this is exactly how the enemy wants us to think about the most powerful news in all the universe. The gospel is a grave danger to him, so if he can lull us into its domestication, he will. The devil is perfectly fine with us holding gospel-centrality *as an idea*.

Keeping the gospel conceptual will leave us vulnerable when temptation comes. Without a firm grasp of the substance of the message and its centrality, we become dried shells, husks of activity where spiritual life should be. We become something along the lines of Jude's portrait of the infiltrating false teachers: "These are hidden reefs at your love feasts, as they feast with you without fear, shepherds feeding themselves; waterless clouds, swept along by winds; fruitless trees in late autumn, twice dead, uprooted" (Jude 12).

The landscape pictured there is dry and dead, a spiritual desert haunted by clouds that give no rain and winds that blow dead branches around like tumbleweeds. It's in such environments that you and I discover what we truly trust to "get the job done." But it's in just such an environment that the center of the gospel signals Christ's strength.

## The Temptation of Efficiency

After the baptism announcing the inauguration of his public ministry, Christ is led by the Spirit into the wilderness to be tempted by the devil (Matt. 4:1–10). For forty days and nights, he endured without food. The hunger pangs at half that duration must have been excruciating. The devil waits until forty days go by, at which point Jesus' body has already begun eating itself. He is the most vulnerable he has ever been, and the tempter suggests something perfectly reasonable: "If you are the Son of God, command these stones to become loaves of bread" (Matt. 4:3).

It is when hunger has become one's normal way of life that the temptation to make bread is most powerful. On day three, four, or five, Jesus would have been hungry, but perhaps the newness of his mission would have helped steel his will. Similarly, in the early days of one's commitment to gospel-centrality, challenges to it are easier to face. Only the most spineless among us would abandon our commitment so soon. As time goes by, however, with no evident fruit manifesting from our ministry strategy, the seeds of doubt begin to sprout. Almost the whole of the problem is that Western evangelicals expect things to "work"—and spirituality is no exception. The new pastor with big dreams for his small church realizes in year two that all of his gospel-centered newness has not grown the church numerically at all. If anything, it has lost a few folks. And his adoption of grace-driven ministry has only elicited a lot of law from his parishioners. This gospel stuff clearly isn't working.

The megachurch leader doesn't feel he has the margin to try the gospel stuff. The church's infrastructure is too complex and too necessarily corporate to focus much on the pastoral. Most of his energy needs to be directed at keeping the organization running smoothly. Lengthy focus on gospel ministry is idealistic and best reserved for the spiritual intensives of staff retreats and other interludes for enrichment. As a normal course of ministry, it just doesn't work.

When interest in growth, productivity, and other visible markers of success supplant biblical emphases, true spirituality suffers. Because true spirituality isn't usually efficient. Real spiritual growth comes from deep roots planted patiently and carefully over a very long period of time.

The devil basically says to Jesus, "*I* know you're hungry. *You* know you're hungry. And we both know you're perfectly capable of snapping your fingers and getting some bread. What are you waiting for?"

But this is not the way. One does not microwave the bread of life.

In fact, so much of Christ's ministry appears frustratingly inefficient. He spends most of his time in small towns and rural areas, interacting mostly with individuals or small groups. Even when Jesus does draw large crowds, he seems to intentionally thin them out or drive them away. And if Jesus committed himself to a ministry of inefficiency, who do we think we are to begrudge that ministry in our own lives?

When the congregation or the pastors or the trustees or the little voices inside our head tell us it's not working, *that's* when we find out if we are gospel people or not.

What many Western evangelicals have decided, in some ways veiled but in many ways not, is that the gospel doesn't rise to the challenges of the day. It is not as powerful, nor as dexterous, nor as versatile as a variety of other rhetorical and ideological strategies available to us for dealing with the myriad cultural and spiritual threats to the church.

## The Temptation of Security

As for threats, the number purported to challenge evangelicals seems to grow exponentially every day. I have often joked with my congregation that if you ever lack things to be afraid of, simply turn on cable news. They will happily supply you with the fears you lack. But most of us do not need the help.

Fearmongering as a galvanizing principle in cultural movements is not new. It's not even just old; it's ancient. Both the pagans and Jewish religious leaders stoked fear to rouse opposition to the early church. The medieval church capitalized on religious fear to distract from its own corruption. Modern fundamentalism in the 1970s–80s stoked fear of everything from computer chips to contemporary Christian music, from heavy metal to He-Man in order to both foment protest and create an alternative consumer marketplace. As long as there have been cultures, there has been a use of fear to guide thinking, solidify sides, and motivate those sides to take action.

To be fair, a great deal of evangelical fear is often justified. I do not mean to suggest otherwise. (The concerns about gay marriage, transgender ideology, and the mainstreaming of perversion being dangerous, especially to children, are not just well founded but perhaps even still *under*-exaggerated.) But there is a reason the most frequent command in all of the Bible is "don't be afraid."

After Satan tempts Jesus at his point of satisfaction, he tempts him at a point of security:

> Then the devil took him to the holy city and set him on the pinnacle of the temple and said to him, "If you are the Son of God, throw yourself down, for it is written,
>
> "'He will command his angels concerning you,'
>
> and
>
> "'On their hands they will bear you up,
>     lest you strike your foot against a stone.'"
>     (Matt. 4:5–6)

This temptation is aimed at compromising the very wonder of the incarnation. For the divine Son to descend to earth and put on flesh was to condescend to us and put on our frailty. The Son does not give up his heavenly power or any of the attributes of his deity, but in his incarnation he opts not to *exploit* them (Phil. 2:6). The normal weakness of the flesh, the vulnerability, is more or less the point. (Contra Athanasius, I do not believe that the sinless second Adam was free of vulnerability to sickness or other physical insecurity.)

Thus, the devil tempts Jesus to pull the rip cord of his divinity. "Why on earth would you subject yourself to this experience?" he is asking. "Aren't you the eternally begotten Son, very God of very God? Yet you're out here in the desert, frail and starving. If you're the Son, act like it."

In this particular approach, the devil is both taunting Christ at his point of sonship—"Prove it," in other words—and probing at his point of weakness—"Protect yourself," in other words.

It is not at all clear that Western evangelicals understand what it means to exist as a minority presence in society, or that they have any wherewithal to tolerate it. This is not the same thing as *liking it*, of course. Only those with a martyrdom complex propose an enjoyment of marginalization or persecution, whether physical or social. (Yet James 1:2 is still in the Bible, as is Matthew 5:11–12.)

No, one need not be glib about the increasing hostility toward Christians and Christianity in the Western world. But we need not be driven to react by fear.

From a place of fear, one often ceases noticing the *imago Dei* in others. The situation is seen as so dire that others must be quickly placed into the category of either friend or foe. When the need for security prevails, we take as friends those whose only commonality with us is their opposition to those we see as foes. And we see as foes anyone whose views are perceived to challenge or even merely unsettle our own.

In the mid-2020s, we are beginning to see tension points emerge among a variety of fear-driven alliances. The liberal left is increasingly at odds with its illiberal factions. One example is the not-at-all-subtle hostility between earlier-wave feminists and modern ideologues of the "gender spectrum" philosophy. In these ideological battles even cultural progressives like tennis great Martina Navratilova, who decries the inclusion of trans women in women's sports, are considered traitors to the cause of liberalism by trans activists and those influenced by them (despite the fact that Navratilova is a lesbian). Harry Potter author J. K. Rowling, herself an avowed feminist, is labeled a TERF—"trans-exclusionary radical feminist"—for affirming the gender binary as well. Rowling writes,

> I've read all the arguments about femaleness not residing in the sexed body, and the assertions that biological women don't have common experiences, and I find them, too, deeply misogynistic and regressive. . . . But, as many women have said before me, 'woman' is not a costume. 'Woman' is not an idea in a man's head. 'Woman' is not a pink brain, a liking for Jimmy Choos or any of the other sexist ideas now somehow touted as progressive.[1]

---

1. J. K. Rowling, "J. K. Rowling Writes about Her Reasons for Speaking Out on Sex and Gender Issues," JKRowling.com, June 10, 2020, https://www.jk rowling.com/opinions/j-k-rowling-writes-about-her-reasons-for-speaking-out -on-sex-and-gender-issues/.

In response, the young cast of the Harry Potter films appeared to fall in line with the opposition,[2] proving that not all those in the performing arts today are entirely comfortable with free speech.

Relatedly, the "old school" classical liberals appear unable (or unwilling) to repudiate the stifling illiberal prejudice being wielded by their ideological heirs on college campuses and on social media, a toxicity that has spread to workplaces and into the general public square. Older and younger liberals may share a unity in opposition to conservatism and perceived conservative "norms" (on gender, religion, race, and more), but the result quite often is the silence of the elders when the youngers vandalize private property, intimidate fellow citizens, or incite riots in alleged protest of, say, a conservative speaker's invitation to address a college club.

On the right, we have seen stress fractures among the "social justice contras"—those political conservatives who quickly allied across religious (and irreligious) and other social lines out of a shared repudiation of a perceived "woke agenda" invading all social spheres. Many Christians were shocked to find among their ranks "election truthers," January 6 apologists, Christian nationalists, and patriarchists advocating the disenfranchisement of women, as well as actual and unapologetic racists. In the anti-woke coalitions, there is growing unease between the "normies" and the "based."

In Neil Shenvi's review of Andrew Isker's *The Boniface Option*, for instance, he writes,

---

2. Abby Gardner, "A Complete Breakdown of the J. K. Rowling Transgender-Comments Controversy," *Glamour*, April 11, 2024, https://www.glamour.com/story/a-complete-breakdown-of-the-jk-rowling-transgender-comments-controversy.

Speaking personally, I understand the frustration of young White men who've spent the last decade watching evangelical leaders sit back or, even worse, pile on while they were being collectively reviled. But the solution to reviling isn't more reviling. My consistent message has always been: we don't have to choose between embracing CRT [Critical Race Theory] and embracing racism; we can reject both.[3]

In the last couple of years, seminary professor Owen Strachan, author of the book *Christianity and Wokeness*, has been called a liberal and, ironically, woke for focusing his ire on racism in the anti-woke dissident right.

Even more recently, the article debate between Carl Trueman and Ben Crenshaw over the relative applicability of the New Testament's political theology to our current context has exposed more rifts among those once previously perceived as ideologically uniform.[4]

This unease is inevitable among all of those who coalesce around a shared insecurity. Fear certainly makes animated bedfellows, but strange ones.

A further twist is just how similar the illiberal left and the anti-liberal right have become in language and even in aims. The ideological lens laid on top of each may be strikingly dissimilar, but authoritarianism is authoritarianism.

---

3. Neil Shenvi, "Toppling Trashworld: A Long Review of Isker's *Boniface Option*," Neil Shenvi—Apologetics, https://shenviapologetics.com/toppling-trash world-a-long-review-of-iskers-boniface-option/.

4. See Carl R. Trueman, "Honorable Conduct in the 'Negative World,'" *Ad Fontes*, May 21, 2024, https://adfontesjournal.com/web-exclusives/honorable -conduct-in-the-negative-world/, a rejoinder to Ben R. Crenshaw, "Nietzscheans in Negative World: A Response to Carl Trueman," *American Reformer*, May 18, 2024, https://americanreformer.org/2024/05/nietzscheans-in-negative-world/.

Illiberalism is illiberalism. In his examination of conspiracy theories propagated among evangelical Christians, Gregory Camp even observes,

> Members of both the political left and right have their own theories concerning a shadowy "Them" who are using their influence and making things happen according to a preordained plan. An irony is that both left- and right-wing groups often point to the same villains.[5]

Many progressives in the United States, protesting Israel's 2023 military incursion into Gaza, sounded a lot like voices on the alt-right with their fearmongering about "Jews" and "Zionists." A humorous video by comedian Ryan Long made the rounds on social media, proposing identical philosophical vocabulary between the left-wing woke and right-wing racists. It features a Woke and a Racist simultaneously saying, "I think we should roll back discrimination laws so we can hire based on race again."[6]

To be driven by fear is functional disbelief in the gospel of Jesus, as genuine belief subdues a fearful spirit (2 Tim. 1:7). For evangelicals specifically, the temptation to find security in anyone or anything outside explicit gospel belief in Jesus creates an in-group and out-group system that threatens unity in the church and fosters reactionary movements at odds with redemptive mission.

The end result is not just a people *literally named for the*

5. Gregory S. Camp, *Selling Fear: Conspiracy Theories and End-Times Paranoia* (Grand Rapids: Baker, 1997), 13.

6. Ryan Long, "When Wokes and Racists Actually Agree on Everything," YouTube video, 1:44, July 20, 2020, https://www.youtube.com/watch?v=Ev373c7wSRg.

*gospel* eschewing the centrality of that gospel to their way of thinking and living, but a blurring of the very meaning of that gospel. In each successive sociological study of such things, we are seeing an increase in the number of "evangelicals" who have no meaningful relationship with a local church or to orthodox Christian doctrine. The 2022 State of Theology survey[7] jointly conducted by Ligonier and Lifeway revealed that 65 percent of evangelical respondents believe people are born innocent in the eyes of God and 56 percent believe God accepts the worship of all religions. Additionally, 43 percent believe Jesus was a good teacher, but not God. And 60 percent agreed with the statement that the Holy Spirit is a force but not a personal being.

Much like the label "gospel-centered," "evangelical" itself has become a political label evincing tribal identity more than subscription to guiding principles.

Perhaps the prevailing fears driving those who once staunchly held to gospel-centrality to instead embrace alternatives are those of losing authority, autonomy, and power.

## The Temptation of Power

One of the most depressing developments of the last few years is just how many professing Christians in the public square seem to find the Bible inconvenient, quaint, and even outdated. A closed Bible makes a fine talisman in the war for Judeo-Christian values, but once opened, it really starts putting a damper on things. This is because the Bible subverts

---

7. The State of Theology, https://thestateoftheology.com/.

our idolization of efficiency and thwarts our desire for security, but mostly because it undermines our self-exalting craving for power.

The temptation of power is a through-line in the original temptation in Genesis 3, as the serpent tests the boundaries of Eve's reliance on God's lordship. "If you eat of the forbidden fruit, you surely won't die," he basically says to her, and in fact "you will become like God" (vv. 4–5, paraphrased).

The tree of course was a regular reminder to the first couple that, for all of their power, for all of their jurisdiction, and for all of their freedom, *they were not God*. Created good and godly, they still had limits.

In the end, Adam forsook the supernatural order of things and made natural the *un*natural. In his attempt to usurp God's rightful exaltation, he falls, and in his falling, so do we.

When Christ comes, then, to set things back to rights, he starts at the bottom, not at the top. Defying centuries of messianic expectation, he does not physically overthrow the foreign occupation of Palestine and reestablish Israel as a theocratic nation (and finally the dominating kingdom over the world). He does not come on a white steed with swords and fanfare; he comes on a donkey under the waving of palm branches.

The spiritual emphases of the Messiah's magna carta—the Sermon on the Mount—reflect the subversion of the worldly order. It is the meek, for instance, who will inherit the earth (Matt. 5:5). Jesus declares that enemies should be given love and blessing rather than vengeance (Matt. 5:38–44). The kingdom belongs not to the powerful, he says, but to the persecuted (Matt. 5:10).

In the desert, the devil tries to derail this mission thusly:

"Again, the devil took him to a very high mountain and showed him all the kingdoms of the world and their glory. And he said to him, 'All these I will give you, if you will fall down and worship me'" (Matt. 4:8–9).

There are two important things worth noting in this temptation. First, all the kingdoms of the world and their glory already belonged to Jesus! He no more needed Satan to grant him those things than he needed a sprinkling of pixie dust to walk on water. As God in the flesh, Christ is the glorious King of all things. Though he was starving and weary in the wilderness, he was simultaneously upholding "the universe by the word of his power" (Heb. 1:3).

Second, notice that Satan equates the worldly power that Jesus explicitly forsakes as a priority of the kingdom with worship of himself. In other words, succumbing to the temptation of power carried out in the spirit of worldliness is nothing less than devil worship.

In the apostolic writings, there is virtually no distinction between "worldliness" and "the spirit of the age," which is antichrist (see 1 John 4:3). Applying these spiritual principles to our modern cultural moment, we must not hesitate then to see Western evangelicalism's craving for power as a great temptation by the spirit of the antichrist.

I believe we see this truth more and more in the outright adoption by professing Christians of worldly attitudes and manners of speaking toward unbelievers and believers alike. The Sermon on the Mount is found increasingly outdated for our modern contexts, out of step with "how things really are." It is perhaps of great value for our spiritual selves but not imminently practical in the realm of "street smarts."

This attitude is first evidenced by the way most of us perceive the Sermon on the Mount as not applying to us or to our specific circumstances. We always aim for the loopholes and try to dodge the conviction.

Why?

Because the Sermon on the Mount decenters us. The kingdom of God runs counter to the way of the world. In the current power economy, as in the ancient, we find this reversal of values to be demoralizing and suffocating to the flesh.

This attitude is also evidenced by the way evangelicals have adopted the world's values in so many of our endeavors. In our gathered worship, we prize theatrics and inspirational moralism. Why? Because these usually accumulate more people—and thus more cultural currency—than the alternative of gospel-centrality. In our politics, we prize haughty voices and authoritarian agendas. Why? Because these are the demonstrations of might we find impressive. In our personal interactions, both virtually and sometimes physically, we mock and insult and humiliate and degrade, despite all the biblical injunctions against such things. Why? Because we envision the "seat of scoffers" (Ps. 1:1) as a royal throne.

Thus, left-leaning evangelicals despise right-leaning evangelicals, right-leaning evangelicals despise left-leaning evangelicals, and those who imagine themselves in the sacred middle disdain them all. Why? Because we all find it difficult to cope with rejection of our viewpoint, which is perceived as diminishing our side's power. We don't mourn or plead so much as we mock and pontificate, because the former are postures of meekness, and we want *power*. We want power unrestrained, unmeasured, and uncontrolled. We want power exerting, actualizing, and dominating. Even if we have to do a little bowing to the spirit of the world (the devil) to have it.

We will even use the Bible to defy the Bible. Just as Aaron tried ascribing the Israelite worship of the golden calf to YHWH (Ex. 32:5), we will appeal to the hard words of Jesus or Paul as license for our harshness toward others. A popular meme states, "When someone asks what would Jesus do, remind them that flipping over tables and chasing people with a whip is within the realm of options." Indeed, and it appears for many to be the primary option.

It does not occur to us, at least not for long, that such hard words could be aimed at ourselves as easily as at the objects of our disgust. In this way, we invert the Bible's commands, applying them always outwardly, never inwardly. We imagine ourselves to be the "holy spirit" of the world, little gods determining who is worthy of favor and who is worthy of condemnation. We exalt ourselves and, like the Miltonic Satan, declare, "Evil, be thou my good."

The temptation of power is a major contributor toward all manner of gospel drift, but when you add it to the temptations of efficiency and of security, you create a siren song for any person or movement who takes their eyes off the glory of the gospel for even a moment. The serpent's garden temptation of Adam certainly proves this.

It's only in Jesus' temptation in the wilderness that we begin to see the precious remedy: the superiority of Christ *who is himself* our righteousness.

## The Tendency to Overcorrect

The landscape of humanity through history is an ever-intertwining web of these three major temptations, and the landscape of contemporary evangelicalism is no exception (though they might manifest themselves in specific ways to different demographics).

When we give in to these temptations, the proper response is always repentance. The Lord's promise is that when we faithfully confess our sin, we will enjoy his faithful forgiveness (1 John 1:9). Therefore, we can at any moment, with the Spirit's empowerment, turn from our idolatrous desires and cravings to the healing of God's glory and grace.

What we usually do instead is defend, deflect, and double down. It seems that every conviction for our sin is met with a self-justifying rebuttal of the sin of another that "caused" ours. "They did it first" is not just the language of elementary school playgrounds and backyard sandboxes; it is the reflexive counterpoint to any evangelical transgression. It will always be so, as long as we crave efficiency, security, and power.

If centering on the gospel requires us to die to our self-centrality, we will try to avoid it.

But there is another way we try to avoid gospel-centrality: overcorrection. It is often deceptive because it is an attempt to bring balance to the landscape of our lives, ministries, and missions. However, a preoccupation with balance casts drift in any direction as an appropriate response to drift in another. (We might consider how overcorrection in driving, especially in hazardous conditions, is one of the most common causes of accidents.)

In religious terms, we often see this in the spiritual navigation of law and gospel. To think along the lines of historic Protestantism, we maintain the right proportion of God's "two words" to us. We proclaim both imperatives (what we're to do) and indicatives (what God does), and we do so in their biblical context and exegetically with their proper biblical emphases. But when we are spiritually disordered, untethered from the Bible's word on law and gospel, we drift into thinking that each is a counterweight to the other.

In the gospel-centered movement, we see these polarized drifts toward either legalism or antinomianism. Those who follow the law perceive an unhelpful emphasis on grace or some practical deficiency in the gospel. They seek not simply to articulate the clear biblical implications of Christ's finished work, but to in essence "move on" from gospel-centrality, to consider the gospel a foundation best kept subterranean. On the other hand, those who perceive the law of God as burdensome denigrate the glory of the law, dismissing it with a kind of "gospel-centered" sleight of hand. I see shades of this approach whenever the concept of church discipline is positioned in opposition to "grace."

The Reformational tradition has historically affirmed the threefold use of the law.[8] The legalistic spirit diminishes the first use, which is to reveal our inability to perfectly fulfill it. The antinomian spirit diminishes the law's third use, which is to give us the imperatives of God-honoring obedience.

When we are influenced unduly by the temptations of

---

8. The biblical law's usage is: (1) as a mirror, revealing the holiness of God and the sinfulness of man, (2) as a curb, useful in the restraining of evil in the world, and (3) as a rulebook, telling us what to do and not to do in order to please God.

efficiency, security, or power, we often think the solution to the problem of one spirit is a good dose of the other. What legalists need to do, we think, is "loosen up." What antinomians need to do is "tighten up."

The problem with this polarity, of course, is that the spirits of both legalism and antinomianism are essentially driven by the same thing: the centrality of self. The legalist may think he is truly honoring God by emphasizing God's law, but he is actually glorifying the righteousness of self. He's implying that the law is actually manageable by sinners who will always stand guilty in the light of it. And the antinomian may think he is truly honoring God by emphasizing God's grace, but he is also glorifying the self, implying that God is not really worthy of our obedience.

Additionally, both legalists and antinomians commit blasphemy against the Holy Spirit—the former by distrusting the spiritual power of grace to empower obedience and the latter by denying said power.

"In the end," Keller writes, "legalism and relativism in churches are not just equally wrong; they are basically the same thing. They are just different strategies of self-salvation built on human effort."[9]

Christ's resolve during the wilderness temptation is again instructive for us. At each point of temptation, he was not sent reeling. He did not find his strength at one point license for weakness in another. No, he stayed focused on the unchanging Word of God.

---

9. Timothy Keller, *Center Church: Doing Balanced, Gospel-Centered Ministry in Your City* (Grand Rapids: Zondervan, 2012), 66.

It is important to remind ourselves of the nature of drift. Extremists aside, no truly Christian preacher makes a definitive, explicit embrace of legalistic or antinomian heresies. Rather, the spirit of these errors can permeate our faith and practice in ways often imperceptible to ourselves and others. As a trainer of aspiring preachers, I remind students that their passion in the pulpit communicates just as much as their rhetoric. As gospel-centered as I may think I am, if over time my hearers can see that my energy, eloquence, and enthusiasm are more heavily marshaled in communication of the law rather than grace, I have embraced a spirit of legalism.

Our emphases give us away. But remaining committed to the basic substance of the gospel-centered paradigm helps us stay anchored to the Scriptures and to the Spirit who has given them to us.

## From Drifting to Anchored

The gospel explodes the competing polarities of legalism and antinomianism. The gospel puts law and grace into their proper proportions—not as two equal weights counterbalancing each other, but as two words from God with biblical dimension and asymmetrical glories.

The Scriptures position the gospel in place of pride. To the legalist, the Bible centers the gospel as the surpassing glory of God in the fulfillment of the law by Christ alone—whose perfect obedience is imputed to the believer by faith—and in the indwelling of the Spirit of God to bear fruit in the Christian's life in accordance with righteousness. It is not the law that trains us to renounce unrighteousness (Titus 2:11–12), but grace. To the antinomian, the Bible centers the gospel as the liberating power of God not just *from* the law but *to* the law, which—in the light of Christ—becomes not a burden but a delight, not a means of merit but a guide to worshipful thanksgiving.

Therefore, the gospel subverts our self-righteous concerns of balance. Pastor and author Adam Mabry writes this about holding apparently paradoxical truths in tension:

> I'm not calling for balance, where you try to hold all things as true at once. Truth cannot be balanced with lies. Jesus didn't "balance" Judaism with Roman paganism, nor did Paul or Peter, who follow him. [And] I'm not talking about some Aristotelian middle way, choosing the best of what both "sides" have to offer and creating our own path. That's just the road to autonomy, and away from biblical authority.[10]

Ironically, such attempts to create a law/grace balance end up only in imbalance. Those who drift toward one way or another sometimes criticize those who seek to put the law/gospel dynamic in its proper biblical tension. The so-called "third-way-ism" of Tim Keller[11] and others is criticized as compromise. It is common among former adherents of gospel-centrality on social media to see repeated criticisms of those perceived to only "punch right" in their evangelical

---

10. Adam Mabry, *Stop Taking Sides: How Holding Truths in Tension Saves Us from Anxiety and Outrage* (Epsom, UK: Good Book, 2020), 13.
11. Keller, *Center Church*, 63–71.

and political positions. Allegedly in response to this third-way compromise, some have adopted a policy of No Enemies to the Right (NETTR). Theologian and ethicist Alastair Roberts comments: "[A] lot of NETTR praxis is purposefully accelerationist. Far-right elements can be desirable allies and associates because they utterly reject the Overton Window and, consequently, are not going to challenge, police, or moderate."[12]

They do not police their side, but they certainly police the opposition!

And if one resists these polarities, seeking to adhere only to the way of Christ, which subverts so much of what is found among both rightists and leftists, one is deemed a de facto leftist, since a "true rightist" would more often "punch left." Even a position of prophetic complaint against "both sides" is often seen as traitorous.

Certainly some do reveal their own drift by focusing their concerns inordinately in the opposite direction. But this tendency is true of those on both the right and the left of any given spectrum. And it is a constant danger for those who think themselves solidly in some alleged "middle."

Those who reject right/left extremes are often accused of adopting a do-nothing neutrality or, worse, embracing a compromising balance, and many of these accusations within the evangelical tribe entail a castigation (and misunderstanding) of Keller-esque "third-way-ism."

Third-way-ists are not immune to drift (in either direction, but perhaps more commonly toward the left). Properly

---

12. Alastair Roberts (@zugzwanged), X (formerly known as Twitter) post, August 23, 2023, https://twitter.com/zugzwanged/status/1694411455381094493.

understood, gospel-centrality is not a "middle way" compromise, balancing between extremes; it is an entirely new category. Just as Jesus does not exist as some pivot between the yin and yang of good people and bad people, the gospel does not exist on a spectrum of spiritualities. Just as the divine Son is God—entirely unique, perfectly holy, and thus wholly *other*—the gospel *is* the spectrum, an entirely other "thing." Thus, the gospel doesn't serve as some theological fulcrum between antinomianism and legalism or between hedonism and moralism; it serves as a theology unto itself standing over them.

For this reason, then, the gospel must be an explicit and intentional tenet of our life and practice. "We have this as a sure and steadfast anchor of the soul," Hebrews 6:19 tells us. Unmoored from the anchor, we may think we are charging forward in valid application of the gospel while unknowingly set adrift from its "first importance" in all things. Therefore, we must pay closer attention to the gospel than we think we must, lest we drift away from it.

In the following chapters, we will examine some forms of drift common within evangelicalism today, even among those who identify as gospel-centered, and see how God's Word can recenter *us* around God's grace.

Chapter Three

# Less than Conquerors

## *A Drift into Victimhood*

*What then shall we say to these things?
If God is for us, who can be against us?*
**—Romans 8:31**

**FOR THE CHRISTIAN, WHAT IS THE INEVITABLE RESULT OF** allowing our sense of identity to be shaped by culture, rather than the other way around?

The critical success of the 2023 film *Past Lives* directed by Celine Song is notable given its quietly subversive take on Western romantic sensibilities. A nominee for Best Motion Picture at the 2024 Academy Awards, *Past Lives* tells the story of Nora and Hae, childhood classmates in South Korea who enjoy an adolescent friendship and perhaps the first signs of puppy love before Nora's family immigrates to Canada. Twelve years later, the two friends reconnect on Facebook, and that puppy love resurfaces. Over a series of video calls, they rekindle their friendship and assuage a bit of the loneliness that each is dealing with in their own way. But Nora is about to move again, to New York this time, and she wants to focus for a bit on starting a writing career, so they take a break from their online meeting. Another twelve years pass.

Nora is now living in New York with her husband, Arthur, when Hae reconnects. He wants to come visit her. Somewhat confused, she agrees. When Hae arrives, Nora shows him around the city and they make conversation along the way, at times awkward, at times deep, catching each other up on the trajectories their lives have taken and, consequently, their *senses of self.*

In the evening, Nora and Arthur take Hae to a bar, where Nora spends most of the evening translating between the two men.

And then the film takes an unexpected turn. In almost every other Hollywood version of this story, Nora would realize that her childhood friend, Hae, is her one true love. Reconnecting after all that time would rekindle the spark long suppressed. In the Hollywood version of the story, the Korean Hae, with all of his life experience and his tortured-soul torch-carrying for Nora would be a much better match for her than her boring Jewish husband. She and Hae would at least sleep together. But that is not what happens.

Instead, Nora politely re-"friends" Hae and pleasantly entertains him. Arthur feels a little like an awkward third wheel in the presence of the childhood friends, but he is respectful and trusts his wife. And while Hae's relational interest in Nora is likely more than platonic, he respects Arthur and never makes a move. In the end, Nora is emotionally moved by the revisiting of her past life, but she is resolutely committed to her current life and her husband. The film ends with a sweet goodbye to Hae as he waits for a taxi to take him to the airport. At this point, the two would customarily share a kiss and fulfill the modern aspirations of romantic cliché. Instead, Nora returns to her apartment and to the arms of her husband.

It is about as anti-Hollywood as a romance film can get. There is no cheating. There is not even any major conflict, except what is happening internally. Whatever pressures the characters may have faced, emotionally or culturally, the result is a sweet ode to tradition, to commitment. As such, *Past Lives* is countercultural in a broken landscape of expressive individualism.

The feminist might argue that Nora should follow her

feelings and embrace her sexual autonomy, her marriage obviously a prison keeping her from living the life she truly wants. The critical theorist might suggest that the Korean Nora could never really be understood by her non-Korean husband and therefore should embrace her heritage by reuniting with Hae. The typical moviegoer simply wants to see more romantic action. In a world where ultimate fulfillment is found in the ultimacy of self, a story like *Past Lives* shouldn't make sense.

In his landmark 1966 book *The Triumph of the Therapeutic*, Philip Rieff pioneered the understanding of Western culture's replacement of traditional religious questions of spirituality with personalized ideals of self-fulfillment. Rieff posits that in a therapeutic culture, questions about salvation cannot be asked in the traditional ways.[1] In the therapeutic, he argues, "there is nothing at stake beyond a manipulatable sense of well-being."[2] The religious considerations of things like heaven and hell, grace and judgment, or salvation and condemnation are not just subjugated to prevailing concepts of self-esteem, self-help, and self-care; they are absorbed by them.

And yet, the import of religious intensity cannot be exorcized from the therapeutic mindset. In fact, the inviolable god of self, it turns out, is just as wrathful as the God of religion. Maybe more so. The therapeutic centering of the self is not simply a perpetual deification; because every person now walks around believing him- or herself to be the center of the universe, we are inevitably and continually aggrieved by everyone else's violations of our sacred self. The therapeutic

---

1. Philip Rieff, *The Triumph of the Therapeutic* (Chicago: University of Chicago, 1987), 6.
2. Rieff, *Triumph of the Therapeutic*, 13.

insistence on self-centrality is by necessity an insistence on victimhood.

## The Rise of the Therapeutic

If it is true that, as Ed Welch argues, "clients tend to drift toward the worldview of their therapists,"[3] American evangelicals have certainly drifted toward the worldview of the therapeutic. Our worship services are characterized by consumerist values. Our sermons are brimming with self-help platitudes. Our bestselling books and most popular podcasts feature the superficial spirituality of prosperity gospel gurus. Our music is less and less theological, more and more "inspirational."

In 2005, sociologist Christian Smith famously proposed that the functional theology of young American Christians amounted to little more than moralistic therapeutic deism. In his study of the spiritual lives of teenagers, he discovered that religious youth are influenced less by the cultural distinctives of historic evangelicalism—to say nothing of creedal Christianity!—and instead more by a benign spirituality, only vaguely Christian, that is perceived primarily as a motivational benefit. The purpose of life, in the moralistic therapeutic worldview, is to be happy and have good self-esteem.[4]

---

3. Ed Welch, "Should Pastors Encourage Secular Therapy? A Guide for Christian Ministry," Desiring God, December 26, 2023, https://www.desiringgod.org/articles/should-pastors-encourage-secular-therapy.
4. Christian Smith with Melinda Lundquist Denton, *Soul Searching: The Religious and Spiritual Lives of American Teenagers* (Oxford: Oxford University Press, 2005), 162–63.

Almost twenty years later, this adolescent spirituality is now the dominant ethos of American evangelicalism.

In the late '90s, Smith's study of evangelicalism more broadly focused in part on the radical individualism endemic to evangelicalism, an individualism committed to differentiation from the wider culture.[5] Some of his conclusions now seem quaint, given the full blossom of this individualism and the incursion into evangelicalism of constant degrading pressures from the outside world. And the dominant pressure is the temptation of power, a very powerful undercurrent in all worldly appeals. The temptation of power in the case of the therapeutic gospel is, like worldly aspirations of power, a desire for self-exaltation.

In his book *Bad Religion: How We Became a Nation of Heretics*, Ross Douthat refers to the result of this corrosive incursion as "God Within" theology. Distinguishing between a specific subculture of the prosperity gospel and the wider influence of therapeutic religion, he writes,

> [A]t the deepest level, the theology of the God Within ministers to a set of spiritual needs, and tries to resolve a different set of contradictions, than the marriage of God and Mammon. Whereas the prosperity gospel suggests that material abundance is the main sign of God's activity in this world, the apostles of the God Within focus on internal harmony—mental, psychological, spiritual—as the chief evidence of things unseen. . . . The prosperity gospel

---

5. Christian Smith with Michael Emerson, Sally Gallagher, Paul Kennedy, and David Sikkink, *American Evangelicalism, Embattled and Thriving* (Chicago: University of Chicago Press, 1998).

makes the divine sound like your broker; the theology of the God Within makes him sound like your shrink.[6]

It is difficult not to see in these analyses everything from the pop psychology of the attractional megachurch "worship experience" to the Jung-meets-MMA posturing of the online Christian "manosphere."

We see it, I think, in the deterioration of evangelical identity altogether, as fewer and fewer professing Christians make church attendance a priority in their regular lives and more and more admitted unbelievers adopt "evangelical" as a political label rather than a religious one.

Building from Philip Rieff's conclusions, Douthat adds,

Religious man was giving way to "psychological man," not ideological man. In place of a secularized Christianity building the kingdom of God on earth, Rieff foresaw an age of therapy, in which the pursuit of well-being would replace the quest for either justice or salvation.[7]

I would argue, in fact, that psychological man has become a new ideological man, as so much of evangelical thinking as it relates to the ideology of faith, politics, and the like is increasingly driven by therapeutic thinking, which is essentially *self-centered* thinking.

The pressing therapeutic influence on contemporary evangelicals is inordinately strong, as it both emanates from

---

6. Ross Douthat, *Bad Religion: How We Became a Nation of Heretics* (New York: Free Press, 2012), 217.

7. Douthat, *Bad Religion*, 231.

the inner desire for power that lies inside every sinner and is echoed by the cultural pressure to become one's "true self," to cast off the shackles of traditional or religious pressures of conformity in order to live one's "best life now." Evangelicals have reliably complained about this messaging, as it's found in everything from Disney cartoons to commercials for soda pop, but we are hardly self-reflective about its presence in our own political ambitions or other cultural engagements. Consider evangelical bestsellers with therapy-influenced titles like *You Be You*; *Do the New You*; and *Clear Mind, Peaceful Heart*. Consider the "you go, girl" self-help inspiration proliferating in evangelical women's spaces online and the "be a real man" macho pump-ups in evangelical men's spaces. Think of the way Republican politicians, backed by evangelicals, live out promiscuous lifestyles and instigate family breakups in the name of living authentically and "telling the truth." The narcissism of therapeutic culture is running amok, and it has seriously infected us.

The effect is a Western culture war typified by an attempt to out-victim the enemy. A dissident right wing with growing sympathy for the thinking of white supremacists employs the same victimhood rhetoric they've for decades accused African Americans of employing.[8] That is admittedly an extreme example, but the sentiment is growing among evangelicals concerned with their ongoing stake in the culture war.

The source of strength then becomes political power,

---

8. Olga Khazan, "How White Supremacists Use Victimhood to Recruit," *The Atlantic*, August 15, 2017, https://www.theatlantic.com/science/archive/2017/08/the-worlds-worst-support-group/536850/.

tribal numbers, and size of influence. I think of how pre-occupied conservative media has become with the numbers at Republican campaign rallies and marches. The influence of therapeutic categories is evidenced in the attempt at justification by affirmation.

The therapeutic identity claims not to look for outside validation. "Nobody is the boss of me!" For evangelicals, it would appear, not even God. Instead, we look to our fellow tribesmen, our factional comrades, for affirmation.

But the snake that lures us in eventually eats its own tail. Even as social contexts tell us to be true to ourselves and that there is no better self than being our best self, we discover there are still particular borders and boundaries at which point these affirmational communities suddenly stop their affirmation. The gay kid who decides he's not gay, or at least doesn't want to be gay out of religious adherence, will find himself excommunicated from the affirming community. The religious fundamentalists who bond over defiance of government lockdown mandates suddenly divide when they discover they have different views on race relations. Even transgressors feel transgressed.

This is the natural result of rooting one's identity in anything other than Christ. The unity is fragile. With self at the center, every disappointment or transgression of the self becomes a capital offense. The victimhood is perpetual.

Ironically, the centering of the self ultimately leads to a profound experience of disorientation, of decentering. David Wells made a deft observation about how rapid changes in media types and media consumption further impact a self-centered culture:

What is striking about the media images themselves is that although they have produced a quantum leap in information and entertainment, they are often little more than a blizzard of rootless, context-free thoughts and pictures. . . . The psychological impression which is made by all of this is that everything is in flux and everything is unstable. These images, which blow around in our minds like leaves in a windstorm, are each discrete, all unconnected, all random, all unregulated, and all uncentered. This is the visual counterpart to the postmodern mentality. Here are decentered beings in their decentered world.[9]

Wells continues,

In a decentered culture, eclecticism is the coin of the realm. This is what excessive choice has done to us. There is simply too much to choose between, ranging from products, to beliefs, to lifestyles, so choice becomes almost random. And the sheer weight of all of the information . . . blurs everything so that one idea seems no truer than another. In this video-commercial context, and in this personal mindset, everything begins to seem similar and equal. Judgements become not only offensive but, for so many, virtually impossible.[10]

As I write this, there are two different—but nevertheless connected—news stories in the national media. In one, young

9. David F. Wells, *Above All Earthly Pow'rs: Christ in a Postmodern World* (Grand Rapids: Eerdmans, 2005), 234–35.
10. Wells, *Above All Earthly Pow'rs*, 235.

activists who militantly align with social justice causes, including radical feminism, anti-racism, and political liberalism, are vocally supporting the cause of the Palestinian terror organization Hamas in their war against the Israelis without showing any hint of recognition that Palestinian Muslim hardliners subjugate women, perpetuate violence against Jews and other ethnic minorities, and advocate for one of the most illiberal conceptions of theocracy on the planet. In the other, university presidents are under fire for their inability to denounce the call for genocide before Congress.

Everything has blurred together. Judgments may not be impossible, but coherent judgments certainly seem so. Some conservative pundits have called this the full effect of the "woke mind virus." It is certainly the result of a bizarre distortion of the therapeutic self, an enthronement of the self, and thus the enshrinement of social laws against violations of the enthroned self. But again, evangelicals have not been immune to this phenomenon. Carl Trueman notes in *The Rise and Triumph of the Modern Self*, "In a world in which the self is constructed psychologically and in which the therapeutic is the ethical ideal, we should therefore expect the notion of good and bad, of what is appropriate and inappropriate behaviors to change accordingly."[11] This premise should apply to the erosion of free speech in the public square as equally as to the erosion of character judgments among evangelicals as they look at their favored public servants.

As we (accurately) perceive a rapidly secularizing West

---

11. Carl R. Trueman, *The Rise and Triumph of the Modern Self: Cultural Amnesia, Expressive Individualism, and the Road to Sexual Revolution* (Wheaton, IL: Crossway, 2020), 326.

that is growing in hostility toward religious liberty, and especially expressions of the Christian faith, we see the threats of marginalization, oppression, and persecution as threats to our very identity. We abandon the teachings of our Lord in favor of fighting back, returning like for like, tit for tat. We willingly adopt the values of the world in our fight against these threats. And while we ought to labor forthrightly to ensure the liberty of conscience and religion in our world, we must not mistake the Christian life in exile as itself an existential threat, lest we inadvertently adopt the culture's self-defeating values of victimhood.

Perhaps nowhere has this victimhood mentality been more prevalent than in the recent evangelical conversations about social justice.

## The Totalizing of Social Justice

It is important to note, first of all, that social concern has always been a part of the evangelical project. "Activism" is one of the components of David Bebbington's famous quadrilateral, enshrined as core to evangelical identity. The nature of evangelical social activism and the kinds of conversations and movements that emerge from it have varied from generation to generation.

In the 1980s into the early 2000s, the abortion issue became the central focus of evangelical social concern. It is an issue that, despite the 2022 overturning of *Roe v. Wade* that sent the question of abortion rights back to the states, remains less of a focus in the evangelical consciousness today. (Three items of note in this regard: Younger white evangelicals poll as less concerned about abortion today than older evangelicals.[12] Only 26 percent of pro-life Republican voters say their preferred candidates for elected office must share their view on abortion.[13] The evangelical abortion conversation over the last few years, especially within the larger denominations, has shown a division among traditional pro-life advocacy and voices in the abortion abolitionist movement, informed by strains of Christian nationalism and theonomy.) In the mid-1990s into the 2000s, groups like Promise Keepers focused explicitly on race relations, a concern adopted across many evangelical denominations without much controversy. In the late 2000s, the success of books like *When Helping Hurts* and the rise of the missional conversation marked an evangelical return to addressing poverty and related systemic issues. These various foci were not without critics, but none sparked a culture-wide battle over ideology, language, and questions of biblical faithfulness.

The year 2016 gave us perhaps the most volatile American election cycle in recent history (which is saying a lot). Shortly thereafter came the increasing unrest over the questions of systemic racism, policing, and justice in general. The lines were quickly drawn, and they ran through whole families, friendships, and churches. Either you support the African American community or you support law enforcement.

---

12. Ryan P. Burge, "What's New in Evangelical Views on Abortion? The Age Gap," *Christianity Today*, January 21, 2022, https://www.christianitytoday.com/news/2022/january/evangelical-abortion-views-age-gap-younger-pro-life.html.

13. Megan Brenan, "One in Four Americans Consider Abortion a Key Voting Issue," Gallup, July 7, 2020, https://news.gallup.com/poll/313316/one-four-americans-consider-abortion-key-voting-issue.aspx.

Either you believe racism has infected every institution and organization since our nation's founding or you believe that systemic injustice is a total myth. In a matter of months, it seemed, one's affirmation or rejection of the concept of "social justice," apparently regardless of any nuance in its definition, became a sign of one's liberalism or one's conservatism.

The era of context and caveats is over. Social justice has become a totalizing force. Your position on social justice, one way or another, proves your allegiance to your tribe of choice.

On the left side of the spectrum, the last few years have witnessed the revivification of the social gospel and liberation theology, a conflating of the biblical good news with social concern in ways that have only served to obfuscate the good news. It is not uncommon to hear these circles sloganeering things like "Social justice *is* the gospel."[14]

Perhaps this is merely the full blossoming of an evangelicalism that has become more social than gospel, more activist than doctrinal. D. A. Carson once noted,

> Some studies have shown that Christians spend about five times more mission dollars on issues related to poverty than they do on evangelism and church planting. At one time "holistic ministry" was an expression intended to move Christians beyond proclamation to include deeds of mercy. Increasingly, however, "holistic ministry" refers to deeds of mercy without any proclamation of the gospel—and that is not holistic. It is not even halfistic, since the

14. Sara Weissman, "Serving the Searching and the Secular," *Inside Higher Ed*, April 28, 2022, https://www.insidehighered.com/news/2022/04/29/seminary-draws-nonreligious-students-social-justice.

deeds of mercy are not the gospel: they are entailments of the gospel. . . . Judging by the distribution of American mission dollars, the biggest hole in our gospel is the gospel itself.[15]

Once we take our eyes off the true gospel, even in a concern about important things, we begin to forget it. I have read over the last few years those ultimately concerned with social issues pontificate on the failures of the gospel-centered movement to go far enough into issues of justice. Once upon a time, we all agreed that the gospel was not merely the ABCs of the Christian life, but the A to Z. Now it seems that some disagree. Where one lands in the social justice conversation tells us what they really believe.

The problem with totalizing the issue this way is that it leads us from social justice concerns to social gospel solutions. What evangelicals who are overly fixated on social justice theorize is an expansion of the gospel's ramifications—which undoubtedly have social effects! But in doing so, they ironically flatten the gospel to a wholly this-world impact. The supernatural power of the good news—and its imparting to us the glory of heaven and a vicarious spiritual conquest of the powers of darkness—is usurped by a moralizing therapeutic that inverts the gospel's relevance. In other words, the prioritizing of social justice obscures Christians' eternality, the preeminence of their heavenly citizenship, and the Bible's directive to "seek the things that are above" rather than things that are on earth (Col. 3:1–2).

---

15. D. A. Carson, *The Gospel and the Modern World: A Theological Vision for the Church*, ed. Brian J. Tabb (Wheaton, IL: Crossway, 2023), 95.

The infusion into the social justice conversation of critical race theory, standpoint epistemology, radical feminism, and the now seemingly ubiquitous LGBTQ+ activism effectively separates everyone into an oppressed-oppressor paradigm. You're either racist or, per the activist's definition, anti-racist. You're an unequivocal ally or you're an enemy.

But this totalization doesn't only happen from one side. Think of what the word *woke* has come to mean in the mid-2020s. Originally a term self-applied within the African American community to refer to the newest iteration of black social consciousness, versions of which we have seen in every decade since the 1960s, it was co-opted by conservative critics and applied to the gamut of social justice concerns. *Woke* is now a pejorative assigned to any whiff of concern about racism, poverty, or injustice. Don't subscribe to the tenets of CRT but believe America's history of institutionalized racism has effects on society today? You're woke. Think liberation theology is heretical but that Christ's teaching obligates us to be concerned for the poor and underprivileged? You're woke.

The victim mentality does not magically dry up once you cross to the right side of the spectrum of views on social justice. When concerns *about the concerns* of social justice become totalizing, the horseshoe theory kicks in, and we see that the two extremes of the conversation are more alike than they realize. Both sides have made a sense of oppression intrinsic to their identity. Both sides are animated by resentment of those thought to be in power and anyone else who refuses to see things the same way. Should it really seem strange to us that following on the heels of social justice, Black Lives Matter, and wokeness is a noticeable resurgence in conservative discourse on antisemitism, racism, and affection for fascism?

The solution to a gospel-deficient social justice concern is not a gospel-deficient *anti*–social justice concern.

## Modern Christianity as Baptized Egoism

Pay attention to how much of the rhetoric in support of Christian nationalism, which is ostensibly predicated on spiritual power and confidence in Christ's rule, is actually driven by a spirit of victimhood. The campaign for this ideology may still be relatively small, but it flourishes on the internet, where performative victimhood itself thrives. And it is expanding into more trafficked media spaces as well. Consider how conservative television pundit Tucker Carlson framed his Christian nationalism conversation with Douglas Wilson as a valid response to Joe Biden's liberal assault on Christianity.[16] "They want to tear down crosses where they can, and cover them up with social justice flags," Donald Trump told the National Religious Broadcasters in 2024. "But no one will be touching the cross of Christ under the Trump administration, I swear to you." He added, "I'm a very proud Christian."[17]

---

16. Tucker Carlson (@tuckercarlson), video on X, April 15, 2024, https://twitter.com/TuckerCarlson/status/1779915085332562039.

17. Will Weissert, "Trump Says He'll Defend Christianity from 'Radical Left' That Seek to 'Tear Down Crosses,'" PBS, February 23, 2024, https://www.pbs.org/newshour/politics/trump-says-hell-defend-christianity-from-radical-left-that-seek-to-tear-down-crosses.

This is not to say that all of the concerns Christian nationalists have about a rapidly secularizing Western world are unfounded! We are seeing regular infringements upon religious liberty and religious speech. Christians are undoubtedly held widely as not just backward but bigoted. The committed evangelical voice on university campuses, in secular workplaces, and in the general public square is treated not merely with marginalization but with increasing open hostility.

The solution, in a (theoretically) democratic society, is not to simply roll over and "take it." With all the legal means at their disposal, evangelicals have every right to oppose infringements upon those rights and to advocate for a society that reflects God's peace and promotes the common good. This includes everything from Christians running for public office to Christians running soup kitchens. What it doesn't include is Christians treating either of those things as the highest purpose of Christian mission in the world.

In some key ways, the focus of evangelicals on this world is very reminiscent of Jewish messianic expectation in the first century. For one thing, both are largely driven by a felt sense of oppression (i.e., a victim mindset) that distorts the perception of Jesus. Among the zealots of Jesus' day, for instance, there was a desire to violently overthrow the Roman occupation and reestablish a biblical theocracy in the land promised to Israel. Is that much different from some evangelicals today openly campaigning for a Christian nation that reintroduces blasphemy laws, abolishes religious liberty for non-Christians, and focuses on national (or even ethnic) identity over kingdom citizenship? When Jesus says his kingdom is not of this world (John 18:36), shouldn't they all feel chastened?

Second, both first-century Jewish nationalism and twenty-first-century Christian nationalism misread the place of oppression (and hardship in general) within the context of God's kingdom. The biblical response to persecution by the powers that be is not to develop a martyr's complex, of course. But there are different kinds of martyr's complexes. There are different ways that a sense of victimhood can inform our identity. It is one thing to lament injustice and to work toward justice; it is another to adopt the personality of one perpetually aggrieved, to live as if one's grievance is the most important thing about oneself. The Bible says so much about justice that to not see it as a valid concern for evangelical ministry would constitute an unfaithfulness to the Scriptures. But nowhere does the Bible bid us to ground our identity in victimhood. If anything, the Bible assumes victimhood as a normal course of life—especially of the Christian life. But grounding our identity in Christ and his finished work gives us the power to persevere, to endure, and even to rejoice.

Third, the embracing of a victimhood mentality inevitably leads to a distortion of Jesus into a projection of one's self-interest. We may deduce that Judas's ultimate betrayal of Christ was rooted not just in greed but in disappointment. He placed his hopes for a different kind of messianic mission upon Jesus and had his dream shattered upon the hard reality of the apostolic ministry. Peter, too, when he unsheathes his sword and assaults Malchus during Jesus' arrest in the garden of Gethsemane, may be acting out of a distorted vision of the kingdom. Today we do the same when we find the way of Jesus inconvenient or frustrating to our religious ideals. Maybe we're following a caricature of Jesus drawn from our own imbalanced view of his teachings, favoring his mercy ministry rather than his clear preaching of judgment or favoring his turning of tables rather than his characteristic gentleness and compassion. In such cases, we make Jesus after our own image. Our Christianity, like early zealotry or pharisaism, becomes little more than baptized egoism. This is the natural result of a self-centered faith driven by a perpetual state of victimhood.

One of the most pressing dangers to gospel-centrality facing the church today is the persistent erosion of security and assurance posed by a prevailing victim mentality. Whether from the woke left or the aggrieved right, lines are often crossed from a sober and realistic assessment of injustice and marginalization to a self-focused identity of victimhood. This has huge implications for our grasp of the gospel—both in our understanding of how Christ's finished work ought to define our sense of self and in our understanding of how to love others, including our enemies.

We may very well be victims of someone's wrongdoing— and the gospel has something to say about that—but the gospel, rightly focused on, also gives us the antidote to a victimhood identity.

## From Victim to Victor

The death of Jesus paid for guilty souls before a holy God. Christ's cross declares justification for sinners. But what does the death of Jesus mean for those who have been sinned *against*?

We currently find ourselves in a strange cultural moment, where flocks of chickens are coming home to roost. Victims of abuse are bravely and boldly exposing the perpetrators of their abuse and in many cases also exposing widespread systemic and institutional injustice in the handling of the aftermath. The Roman Catholic Church and city governments. Jerry Sandusky and Penn State. Larry Nassar and Michigan State. Harvey Weinstein and Hollywood. And the evangelical church has not been immune to incidents of abuse or institutional mishandling of the aftermath.

What rises to the surface in the Christian's understanding of these matters is often a superficial perception of the complexities of pain, shame, pathology, and injustice. A sentimental theology will not do. "Let go and let God" will not do.

And when speaking to victims—whether of abuse or any other number of less traumatic yet still painful sins—we certainly cannot represent Christianity as a Band-Aid. The cross of Jesus is simultaneously a place of immense grace and a place of immense wrath. It is a place of excruciating pain but also exhilarating promise.

The Bible does not treat the atoning work of Christ as one-note. The primary thing it does is reconcile sinners to a holy God who loves them, but there is a ripple effect from the atonement to waters still deeper than many Christians seem willing to go.

The gospel of Jesus can in fact turn victims into victors:

Who shall separate us from the love of Christ? Shall tribulation, or distress, or persecution, or famine, or nakedness, or danger, or sword? As it is written,

"For your sake we are being killed all the day long;
we are regarded as sheep to be slaughtered."

No, in all these things we are more than conquerors
through him who loved us. (Rom. 8:35–37)

There is certainly a victimization referenced in these verses, but the emerging identity in verse 37 is not one of victim but of victor. The cross of Christ secures our identity from victimhood.

Now, please understand this: I am not saying sufferers of abuse or other sins are not victims. The cross does not secure us from victimization. If anything, Jesus promised more trouble to Christians on top of the regular trouble that comes with living in an evil world. The cross does not secure your body from victimization. But it does secure your identity from victimhood.

Victimization is what happens to you; victimhood refers to your state of being. You can be a victim and yet not ground your identity in victimhood. To identify as a victim is necessary for healing. In fact, many sufferers of abuse experience long delays in even reckoning with what happened to them because many have been led to believe—by their abusers or by others around them—they are not victims. So we cannot proceed with any kind of comfort or healing without accurately dealing with what actually happened. To deny victimization is in fact to treat sin with less seriousness than the Bible does.

Nevertheless, for a victim to ground their identity in victimhood is to delay healing. Why? Because grounding your identity in victimhood is a way of letting those who've sinned against you define the terms of your identity. You give them the power of not just hurting you but also defining you. You should not define yourself by what was done *to* you but rather by what was done *for* you.

The bit of poetry in Romans 8:36 is Paul quoting from Psalm 44:22. Psalm 44 is a lament, the kind of song you might sing if you were in so much pain and trouble you might be tempted to think God doesn't love you anymore, or maybe even believe there's not a God at all. One line in Psalm 44 basically asks if God is sleeping. That's how abandoned the psalmist feels.

The apostle Paul then brings this feeling into the crosshairs of the gospel of God's love.

When you feel utterly hopeless, like redemption will never come, what do you do? What have you got left?

It's not unchristian to feel hurt because of wrongs committed against you. It's normal. Normal people feel sad about sad things. Normal people feel bad when others hurt them. There's nothing unchristian about being hurt by injustice. It would be unchristian if we didn't care!

But what Christians cannot do is define themselves by their feelings. This is the therapeutic self at the center; that is, our ultimate validation found in self. Nothing in Romans 8:35–37 indicates that our identity rises or falls on our circumstances or how we feel. In fact, the gospel truths of Romans 8 defy the power of our circumstances. They defy the pain of our bodies or spirits.

But we must lay hold of this truth! We must refuse to be defined by what has happened to us. This doesn't mean we ignore it or whitewash it or pretend like it never happened.

It doesn't mean we shouldn't pursue justice when necessary. But it does mean we should refuse to be defined by our victimization. The Christian's identity in Christ is not one of victimhood but one of victory. We don't even have to feel at peace for this to be true. Notice that Paul says, "*In* all these things we are more than conquerors" (Rom. 8:37), not *out of* them. Because of "him who loved us" (Rom. 8:37), we can be in the midst of some very painful things and yet still have the benefits of Christ's conquest of the powers of death and injustice, because abusers don't own your soul and abuse doesn't have the final word. You may be a victim, but because of the cross, you are also a victor, like Jesus, who conquered the very sin perpetrated against him in his death on the cross.

When I am tempted to see infringements upon my rights as existential threats to my identity, I think of the great multitude in Revelation 7 who have come out of the tribulation. Do you realize that in the economy of the kingdom, the persecuted are the most powerful people who exist?

In the economy of the kingdom, we see how the gospel empowers victims to overcome their circumstances, experience peace, and even extend love to enemies and forgiveness to those who've wronged them.

When we focus on the gospel, our victim mentality vanishes and the power of joy, even in the midst of suffering (Col. 1:24), overtakes us.

Chapter Four

# Less than Delight

## *A Drift into Dryness*

*Their heart is unfeeling like fat,*
*but I delight in your law.*
**—Psalm 119:70**

FOR THE LAST FIVE YEARS I'VE CONDUCTED ONLINE MINISTRY coaching cohorts for pastors wanting to improve their grasp of gospel-centrality. We usually spend a couple of months on the subject of preaching, and the number one question that comes up in these forums is this: "How can I make sure to preach Christ and his gospel every single week, in every single sermon, without it feeling routine?"

The concern is that preaching Jesus will begin to feel formulaic, a kind of homiletic formality. The sermon will center on a different biblical text each week, but—surprise, surprise—"it's all about Jesus."

I sympathize with these pastors' concerns. There is certainly a way that gospel-centrality awkwardly applied can result in a mundane formula that over time fails to captivate. There are also a number of resources available that help to facilitate against a cookie-cutter rigidity in Christ-centered exposition. I have found the work of Sidney Greidanus and Graeme Goldsworthy particularly helpful here, as they have highlighted the variety of sound exegetical options in preaching Christ from every text. Resources from these men, and from a growing number of others, can help the sincere preacher faithfully exposit the Scriptures while "finding the road"[1] (to use Spurgeon's metaphor) from the text to Christ.

But I sometimes doubt lack of exegetical know-how is the root of the problem. I suspect the reason many preachers

---

1. Charles Spurgeon, "Christ Precious to Believers," in *Sermons of the Rev. C. H. Spurgeon of London* (London: Robert Carter and Brothers, 1883), 356–57.

struggle to preach Christ in passionate ways is because they struggle to feel a passion for Christ themselves. The problem is not one of hermeneutic, but one of heart.

I recall that when I was fairly new to the practice of gospel-centered preaching I heard this voice in my ear over and over trying to convince me that preaching the gospel every single Sunday would get boring. I came to identify that voice as belonging to the devil. The problem is that I occasionally heard this complaint from actual people in my congregation. "Sometimes we just need to hear other things," a lady said to me once.

During the heyday of the gospel-centered movement, there were many leaders ascribing to it the label of revival or renewal. Some hailed it as a new Protestant Reformation. (In 2009, *Time* magazine even listed the "New Calvinism" as one of the 10 Ideas Changing the World.[2]) The hope of many and the belief of some was that there was a fresh movement of God restoring theological order and, through it, missional zeal to the evangelical church. For many individual believers and individual churches, this was indeed the experience. For a great many others, however, gospel-centrality has proven to be merely the latest in a series of flash-in-the-pan marketing opportunities.

I had a friend from the early days of gospel-centrality who worked on a behind-the-scenes team of one of the largest resource ministries. He was a vocal and passionate supporter of all our tribe's celebrities. But as the movement began to wane and as more and more of our celebrities proved to be

---

2. David Van Biema, "The New Calvinism," *Time*, March 12, 2009, https://content.time.com/time/specials/packages/article/0,28804,1884779_1884782_1884760,00.html.

fallible (and in some cases fallen) men, he moved his voice and passion to the emergent church space, starting a podcast to stump for more progressive causes. These days he is active in the post-deconstruction exvangelical spaces. Did he ever truly believe? I don't know. But watching the every-few-years shift to a new movement makes me wonder if he was won more to a cause than to Christ.

What makes the difference?

Those most committed to the principles of gospel-centrality are not those who have intellectually assented to them but those who have had a profound *felt experience* of them. In other words, gospel-centrality did not simply change their ministry strategies. It changed their lives.

One of the biggest dangers facing Christians today, given all we have to set in front of our eyes, is flat-out *boredom* with the gospel. It is not so much a misunderstanding of Christ's finished work that poses a danger but more a lack of delight in it. Even in our churches, we often seek out entertainment and frivolity.

Despite all the energy and zeal shown in the public sphere by evangelicals ostensibly committed to biblical truth, I do not think evangelicalism as a culture is particularly known for its spiritual vitality. We are recognized for our religious commitments. We are certainly known for our political stances. But despite all of our resources, gifts, and history, we find a spiritual apathy pervasive among us.

To be overstimulated and yet underwhelmed is a grave danger to a church in desperate need of revival. But the gospel, persistently stared at, can give us the antidote to spiritual dryness.

## Disordered Instincts

Underneath a pastor's sermon preparation and eventual sermon delivery runs a current of instincts and impulses. This current can run in the direction of Christ, or it can run in the direction of a thousand other things the pastor (or their congregation) finds of interest. Today the homiletic instincts of evangelical preachers run the gamut from political hobbyhorses and culture warriors to historical lecturers and theological bromides. Perhaps the most widespread passion of evangelical preachers is the law, whether of positive moralism (the attractional church) or expositional imperativeness (the self-consciously Protestant church). But you can also find in many independent churches a kind of preaching that is just thinly veiled gossip—rants about other churches, other ministries, or even the sinners in that very congregation. It just so happens that this is also many congregations' favorite genre of sermon. Is it any wonder that so many evangelical preachers find the routine of gospel-centrality shallow or mundane? It is not nearly as entertaining as the alternatives. It does not hold much promise of keeping the customers satisfied.

But for the man whose soul has been turned inside out by grace, none of this really matters. In his right mind, he is not interested in his approval rating. Focused on the glory of Jesus, he actually cannot think of a more beautiful, more glorious, more captivating subject. Nor can he think of a more versatile, multifaceted, eternally interesting subject!

In his book *Preaching*, after a series of hermeneutical suggestions to the preacher on how to communicate Christ from every text of Scripture, Tim Keller finally recommends "preaching Christ from instinct."[3] It's a concept I first heard him reference in his talk "What is Gospel-Centered Ministry?" delivered at the inaugural conference of The Gospel Coalition in 2007.[4] In the middle of his now-legendary typological sequence—"Jesus is the true and better . . ."—he interjects the comment, "That's not typology; that's an instinct." He goes on to say, "Until that instinct shows up in your sermons, all you will present are lectures, not sermons."[5]

What is Keller talking about?

I do not believe he is speaking of the tendency of some to treat Christocentric reading of the Bible as a kind of haphazard "Where's Waldo?" experiment. In fact, Keller was giving examples of a typological hermeneutic. I think he is saying that until the preacher himself is personally captivated to the point of delight in the gospel of Jesus Christ, his efforts at inserting the gospel into his preaching will frequently feel to him and to his audience like mere methodological formulas.

Ed Clowney writes, "Since a homiletician named Carpzovius produced a volume of one hundred sermon plans three centuries ago there has been no lack of sermon methods. But biblical theology is not a method in this sense. If its principle is grasped, it cannot be optional or superficial."[6]

---

3. Timothy Keller, *Preaching: Communicating Faith in an Age of Skepticism* (New York: Penguin, 2016), 86–90.

4. Tim Keller, "What Is Gospel-Centered Ministry?" The Gospel Coalition, video, 55:25, May 28, 2007, https://www.thegospelcoalition.org/conference_media/gospel-centered-ministry/.

5. Keller, "What Is Gospel-Centered Ministry?"

6. Edmund P. Clowney, *Preaching and Biblical Theology* (Phillipsburg, NJ: P&R, 2002), 87.

Yes! Gospel-centrality can be a preacher's artifice, or it can be a preacher's awe. The instinct to get to the good news in our preaching and teaching will never come from a superficial application of the gospel as a "technique." The instinct can only come from the preacher's intimate communion with the person of the living Christ.

## Gospel-Centrality versus Spicy Bits

The negative impact of using the gospel as a technique probably cannot be overstated, despite the fact that its appearance is often very subtle. Sometimes a ministry leader's drift into spiritual dryness is not readily noticed because the leader is otherwise very passionate, eloquent, and dynamic. Sometimes there is a rhetorical sleight of hand at work. The leader excels in capturing attention in other key ways, each acting as a misdirection from its brittle connection to the gospel.

If this weren't true, we would not be so shocked when a leader known for their strong sense of doctrine and their public commitment to the gospel commits a catastrophic moral failure. Reviewing some of the endorsements of Paul David Tripp's *Dangerous Calling* is a window into past commitments to gospel-centrality and a window into present apostasy.

For those edgy leaders still plugging away in their ministry careers, we sometimes see shifting emphases and commitments, outsized personalities, or niche controversies supplanting routine delight in the gospel as their stock-in-trade.

I'm reminded of John Piper at a conference panel over a decade ago complimenting Doug Wilson's prophetic sarcasm while warning him about his trademark acerbic wit. There need to be "more obvious tears" in your work, he said.[7]

What actually made the prophets of old *prophets* was not that they said offensive things and threatened judgment and pronounced woes all over everything; it's that *they actually knew God*. Their hard edges came from rubbing shoulders with the glory of the eternal Holy One of Israel. And they weren't all hard edges. They wept over their cities. They felt in their guts the lostness and the compromise they confronted. Idolatry wasn't just offensive to them; it was heartbreaking.

We cannot develop these instincts when the gospel is served as a side dish in our buffet of religious media. We cannot develop these instincts without a relational closeness to Christ, who felt compassion for the crowd of unbelievers.

There is a subset of Reformed evangelicals who spend the bulk of their time online LARPing as prophets, criticizing their perceived enemies and mocking the lost. They think sitting "in the seat of scoffers" is the place of the blessed (Ps. 1:1). Why? Because their Jesus is a caricature. They like his table-turning and demon-casting, but they know little to nothing of his kindness, gentleness, and love for the unclean.

---

7. "Mohler, Piper, Sproul, and Wilson: Questions and Answers #1," recorded at the 2000 Ligonier National Conference, YouTube video, 34:25, July 26, 2013, https://www.youtube.com/watch?v=lnBCeCJzJSc&t=1442s.

There is a subset of Reformed evangelicals who've made opposition to empathy their whole personality. Sober-minded evaluation raises the alarm. Why?

Because anything that becomes "our thing" that isn't the *main thing* is in actuality a boring thing. And because filling our sermons and ministry with assorted "spicy bits" sometimes masks the spiritual dryness of our relationship with Jesus. British writer Monica Baldwin, a former nun, once commented on the boring preachers of the 1940s:

> After long reflection, I have come to the conclusion that this spiritual dullness must be the outcome of having little or no 'personal relations'—if that is the proper name for it—with God. The boring preachers were those who, instead of discussing God's ways and works as a man speaks about the doings of his friend, dished up second-hand material and served it up with rhetoric as sauce to hide the staleness of the taste. Just the difference between someone who reads aloud extracts from a book of travels and somebody who has actually visited the spot.[8]

Baldwin found the preachers who wanted to serve up some "sizzle" to be the boring ones.

We must take care that our commitment to the gospel isn't merely ideology. If so, it will not last. Our preaching will feel boring when we get to the gospel. It will feel routine when we get to Jesus. And worse: we will set ourselves up for

---

8. Monica Baldwin, *I Leap over the Wall: A Return to the World after Twenty-Eight Years in a Convent* (London: Pan, 1958), 229.

spiritual disaster if we commit to a gospel in public that we do not regularly enjoy in private.

If we do not find the gospel glorious, we will become hungry for other things that promise to satisfy. But if we regularly feast on Christ, we will lose our taste for anything else.

A regular and fervent fixation on Jesus (Heb. 12:2 NIV) can make more obvious to us distractions like these:

- Political rants departing from faithful exposition of the text.
- Long and detailed ruminations on exegetical minutiae that masquerade as biblical "depth."
- Camping out on all the sins found *outside* the church walls.
- Self-indulgent creative storytelling in place of true expositional preaching.
- Hot-topic soapboxing and "preaching to the choir" that scratches a congregation's itching ears.
- Softening the rough edges of Scripture, downplaying key doctrines under the banner of "seeker sensitivity."
- Self-righteous polemics.
- Intellectual exercises that substitute for spiritual exhortations.

There are in fact a great number of things preachers and teachers have used over the years to either replace or give the impression of genuine affection for Jesus. And the more time we spend with the real Savior, the more allergic we will become to false saviors.

# Spiritual Vitality and Friendship with Jesus

If you ask any Christian who has experienced a serious moral failing what started their decline from compromise into sexual immorality or another disqualifying sin, they will invariably tell you it began the day they stopped communing with Jesus. One former pastor who wrecked his marriage and ministry with an "emotional affair" outlined the start of his drift this way:

> These problems all started when I failed to rightly respond to some difficult trials in my life. Dealing with them in a biblical way would have included helpful things like repenting from deep-seated heart idolatry and seeking counsel for marriage problems.
>
> An example of the former is that I've realized pastoral ministry was an idol to me in a sense—a lot of my motivation for pursuing holiness, loving my wife, and staying away from temptation came from being a pastor. Why had I always followed the rule of never spending time alone with a woman but then broke it after so many years of ministry? It was because I no longer had the motivation of loving my job and wanting to stay far away from anything that could ruin it. But from the start, I should have kept myself from tempting situations only because of a love for Christ and others, not because I wanted to remain a pastor. Even good things can become dangerous idols if we're not careful, and the ways Satan and the flesh make use of our trials can be very subtle

and clever. I externally fulfilled my pastoral calling with competence, but I had allowed my personal walk with God to grow cold.[9]

This pastor's affair did not begin with an amorous quest for sexual gratification. It actually began when he became spiritually lazy.

I find it strange that so few ministry leaders in the gospel-centered tribe even speak about Jesus in personal terms. I suppose some would say this is out of respect. We are not to speak casually about the second person of the Trinity. He may be the friend of sinners, but he is the King of Kings and the Lord of Lords. He is the risen Son and the imprint of the very nature of God.

But he is also our brother, our Advocate, our Prince of Peace, and our Good Shepherd. Because of his gospel, we are privileged to become partakers of his divine nature (2 Peter 1:4). Shouldn't our communication about Jesus regularly indicate this kind of spiritual intimacy?

Many of those who go through long periods of spiritual drought do not readily feel it, because of the sedative effect of religious interest. Perhaps they even think about Jesus or study things about him. Like the dying man in the desert, they see an oasis and believe they are saved. Until their body cannot go any farther.

In his *Institutes of the Christian Religion*, John Calvin warns against theoretical interest, purely intellectual

---

9. Jim Newheiser, "Lessons Learned from a Fallen Pastor," Biblical Counseling Coalition, December 2, 2020, https://www.biblicalcounselingcoalition .org/2020/12/02/lessons-learned-from-a-fallen-pastor/.

ruminations on the things of the gospel. He calls such exercises "frigid speculations."[10]

The truth is that no amount of religious interest, ministry effort, or other kinds of spiritual enthusiasm can serve as a substitute for actually knowing and spending time with Jesus. Even a rigorous interest in God's law cannot replace communing with God in Christ. To love Jesus is to obey his commandments, yes (John 14:15). But it's possible to obey his commandments without loving him. Just think of the way you sometimes follow your boss's orders or, for that matter, the way your children sometimes follow yours. Is the heart always in it?

John Owen said this about apostasy and what keeps sinners from drifting into it:

> Love of the truth and experience of its power in the hearts of men will produce this effect, and nothing else. All other means where these have been wanting have failed in all places in the world, and will do so again when a time of trial shall come. True religion may be established by law, countenanced by authority, have a prescription of a long profession, or be on other accounts so fixed on the minds of men, as that multitudes shall promise the firmest stability in the profession thereof. But there is no security in things of this nature; and we shall quickly see all the hopes that are built upon them vanish into nothing.[11]

---

10. John Calvin, *Institutes of the Christian Religion*, 1.1.12 (Philadelphia: Westminster, 1960), 100.

11. John Owen, *Apostasy from the Gospel*, in *The Complete Works of John Owen*, vol. 14 (Wheaton, IL: Crossway, 2023), 192.

Religiosity cannot ultimately keep us from apostasy. If anything, it might expedite it, as we find it harder and harder to keep up the religious efforts without a renewed heart. The machinery of "spirituality" cannot move for long without the oil of spiritual vitality. And this spiritual vitality can come only from friendship with Jesus.

After over three decades as a follower of Jesus, I've come to believe that most followers of Jesus will not go substantially deeper in their relationship with him until they've actually drifted into dryness to the point of catastrophe. This was certainly true for me. When the rottenness of my life of sin (pornography) could not stay hidden, the religious facade I'd carefully crafted as a subterfuge against being known catastrophically crumbled. My wife didn't want to be married to me. I couldn't find a ministry position that would have me. And I entered the darkest depression of my life. A decade of accumulated tips and steps from my time in attractional ministry didn't help. And while I wish I could do it all over again to avoid all of the pain and heartache, I can see now that it was exactly what I needed to discover the satisfying beauty of Jesus as my all in all. Like those Paul is speaking to in 1 Thessalonians 1:6 who "received the word in much affliction," at the intersection of personal bankruptcy and the riches of Christ, I discovered "the joy of the Holy Spirit."

It's sad to say, but for most of us, Christ does not become our only hope until Christ becomes our only hope. I want you and me both to avoid a drift into the kind of spiritual dryness that degrades our spiritual health and the glory of our God. But I'm conscious of the fact that many of us must hit the bottom before we'll look up.

Spiritual vitality does not result from talking a lot about Jesus. It does not result from focusing on Jesus as a moral exemplar. It won't even result from talking a lot about spiritual vitality!

When you have come to the end of all of this. When the paradigm of gospel-centrality has seemed to wear out its usefulness and you've moved on to "deeper," more practical, more relevant, or more allegedly vital things. When you've finally used up all of your time and energy with things that seemed to matter more than anything but only left you feeling empty, angry, tired, and lonely. When glomming on to the next ministry strategy feels too daunting, too difficult, or too dang dumb. When the sin you're medicating against with all your ministry efforts can't and won't stay hidden any longer. When you have failed. Then! There is Christ, steady as always. He has never left you, and he is mighty to save.

Then you may find what you'd been denying all along: Jesus is the friend of sinners.

Yes, even your friend.

Now, then: Do you think that's something boring?

Chapter Five

# Less than Deep

## A Drift into Superficiality

*. . . that Christ may dwell in your hearts through faith—that you, being rooted and grounded in love, may have strength to comprehend with all the saints what is the breadth and length and height and depth . . .*
**—Ephesians 3:17–18**

IN 2009 WHEN I WAS WORKING FOR THE DOCENT RESEARCH Group, providing freelance research assistance for a few different pastors across the country, one of my clients was a fellow who pioneered the use of movie clips in Sunday sermons. Part of my getting to know him entailed attending a service at the campus of his multisite church nearest to me to get a feel for their ministry philosophy and style. I happened to attend while they were in the middle of a "God at the Movies" sermon series.

Upon arrival, I settled into a seat in a surprisingly small video venue that looked like it had been a bar or country-and-western club in a previous life. That Sunday's featured film was *The Bucket List*, the 2007 comedy starring Jack Nicholson and Morgan Freeman. I expected the sermon would cover a particular theme or topic, and a film clip or two would be shown illustrating that theme or topic. I discovered the exact opposite. Multiple lengthy clips from the movie were shown, and after each, the preacher (on video) would appear to comment on the clip and what we could learn from it.

The film was the text of the sermon; the exposition was not of the Scriptures, using the film as illustration, but of the movie itself. The entire production felt slick, stylish, and . . . hollow.

I spent over a decade in seeker-sensitive churches, where I was originally trained for ministry. I witnessed firsthand the focus of this ministry movement changing over time from reaching the unchurched to entertaining the overchurched. Church music became more theologically bland. Sermons got shorter and a lot less biblical. The gospel went from a surprise feature at the end of a service to an odd curio reserved for special occasions. In an effort to maintain "relevance," the seeker church gradually began to embrace the superficiality of the consumerist culture it was trying to reach.

In one church we attended, over consecutive weeks of worship gatherings, the service would begin with the band performing a song from pop radio before launching into a "worship set" of songs that would not mention God, followed by a thirty-minute "sermon" that didn't mention Jesus. I began wondering if the notable absence of Christ and his gospel from the proceedings was by design, rather than just out of ignorance.

What was once called the "seeker-sensitive church" has now morphed into thirty-one flavors of consumeristic choices, all operating under a banner often called "attractional." The point of the attractional church is, naturally, to *attract*. There are many different kinds of attractional churches, but the common denominator among them is the embrace of a consumerist ethos and a pragmatic methodology (more on that later) in an attempt to "reach people."

Important to note in the development of this phenomenon over the last century is how dependent it is on cultural influence. And over the last century, the dominant influence has undoubtedly been youth culture. How did this transitory period of the human lifespan become the prevailing influence on American culture and, by extension, the American church?

Scholar Thomas Bergler calls this concept, now a generational phenomenon, "the juvenilization of American Christianity." In his book of that name, he writes,

Juvenilization is the process by which the religious beliefs, practices, and developmental characteristics of adolescents become accepted as appropriate for Christians of all ages. It begins with the praiseworthy goal of adapting the faith to appeal to the young. But it sometimes ends badly, with both youth and adults embracing immature versions of the faith.[1]

The commitment of the American church to the values of youth culture, and worldly culture in general, has kept us in a perpetual state of superficiality. This situation has become even more dire as the developments in technology over the last twenty years or so have curbed the average American's ability to read, listen, and think deeply, which has massive impacts on a person's theological commitments, biblical literacy, and spiritual maturity. When we uncritically wed consumerist culture to the Christian community, it is not the culture that becomes more Christian, but the Christian who becomes more cultural.

## Christianity as Performance Art

In the early years of my figuring out this whole "gospel-centered thing," there was a significant rival for my spiritual and ministerial attention—the so-called "emerging church." The emerging church conversation seemed to be led entirely by people of my generation, while the gospel-centered

---

1. Thomas E. Bergler, *The Juvenilization of American Christianity* (Grand Rapids: Eerdmans, 2012), 4.

movement was led mostly by men my father's age or grandfather's age. On top of that, emerging church leaders were actively engaged in the then-labeled "missional conversation," and this was of great interest to me as a young pastor. I was very invested in leading my church to think of itself as a missionary people.

Further, I was intrigued by the way emerging church leaders spoke of cultural engagement rather than cultural appropriation. As a creative, I was also very interested in a more meaningful way of cultivating artistry in the church that had cultural resonance. Burned out on happy-clappy contemporary Christian music and the baubles and trinkets that passed for Christian art in our subculture, I found the vision in the emerging church movement for patronage of the arts, a return to historic aesthetics, and creativity with depth and quality to be greatly appealing. (While I was working as a church planter, I was also trying to build a career as a novelist.)

The emerging church should have been an easy cultural fit since I, too, felt like I was emerging from an evangelical subculture I was largely rejecting. But for the life of me, I couldn't quite figure out what the movement was emerging *into*.

My confusion began when I first saw the NOOMA teaching videos featuring Rob Bell. I had been invited as a potential teacher into my attractional megachurch's college and twentysomethings ministry, which at the time was meeting in our tech director's living room. The NOOMA videos were hip, artsy, and provocative. In each video, Bell followed up a parabolic story or intriguing cultural illustration with a bit of teaching that always seemed to leave more open than resolved. He always asked more questions than he provided possible answers. And he hardly ever referenced the Bible (except maybe to talk about how Christians had misunderstood it). I came to appreciate the production quality of the videos while finding the messaging rather thin—all style, no substance. It occurred to me that this kind of production wasn't really any different from the seeker church production it aspired to differentiate from.

I read Donald Miller's *Blue Like Jazz*, a bestselling book that occupied a lot of attention among Christians of my generation. Miller seemed to speak a language that Gen-X evangelicals could finally understand, raising uncomfortable questions and probing discomfiting tensions too many of our elders were afraid to address. I was full of angst myself, both about evangelicalism and about life in general. But despite the fact that I liked grunge music and enjoyed books by experimental, "indie"-style authors like Dave Eggers and David Foster Wallace, *Blue Like Jazz* didn't grab me at all. I could appreciate the style, but I longed for substance.

Despite being a young creative deeply interested and personally invested in the arts, I found myself much more drawn in those days to old, "nerdy" men like John Piper, D. A. Carson, R. C. Sproul, and Tim Keller. I had eaten, slept, and breathed enough of the superficiality of the attractional church to know a repackaged version for the grunge generation when I saw it. If anything—believe it or not—the seeker churches I'd been a part of were more theological, less shallow than the avant-garde emerging church stuff that was promising more rootedness, more depth, and more "authenticity."

The last pastor of that megachurch we'd been a part of (before I left with much of the twentysomething ministry to plant an independent church) was heavily influenced by Rob Bell. He had been on staff at our pioneering seeker church Willow Creek in South Barrington, Illinois, but had gradually come to reject what he saw as the modern rudiments of conventional faith. His Sunday teaching became the last straw for my family in leaving, as we witnessed the devolution of messaging from occasionally biblical to only vaguely spiritual. After we left, this pastor led a church of thousands to the point of closing its doors and selling its property. He relaunched a new church in the same city built entirely around "rethinking the faith," where questions were more important than answers, and all persons were affirmed no matter their views or convictions.

This apostasy is the natural consequence of Christianity as performance art. And Christianity as performance art is the natural consequence of the gospel being supplanted by the idol of cultural relevance.

## The Rise of Christianity as "Content Creation"

The idols of cultural relevance and performative faith have made significant inroads among those who once held (or still claim to hold) the principles of gospel-centrality. The social media "influencer" phenomenon has shaped new iterations of evangelical attempts at treating church like a marketable consumer good. Where gospel-centered folks once maintained a healthy aversion to the cultural-relevance-at-all-costs mentality of the attractional church, we now see more drift back into positioning the church as a product.

We see this manifested not just in the creative trappings of sermon series and produced worship arts and the use of online media, but in the very way faith is communicated in sermons and biblical teachings. This is especially evident in the increasing treatment of sermons as "packaged content." The reframing of spiritual communication as a product categorized as "content" is a direct pull from the digital age of the creative, but its indiscriminate employment by churches has severely eroded evangelicalism's intellectual integrity and pastoral sensibility.

Take, for instance, the way sermons are increasingly treated as mines for viral video moments or simply as consumer products as a whole. With the growing acceptance of video venues and satellite campuses, more and more preachers are treating their preaching as a performance for the masses, rather than a well-hewn word for a specific flock. The sermon is treated like a curated consumer good, informed by committees acting like customer focus groups and contributed to by teams of writers. The sermon becomes a package of content designed for ease of distribution. Because of this reimagining of the preaching event, we are even seeing increasing transferability of sermons between churches, which can cause issues with plagiarism.

In 2021, it came out that Ed Litton, then president of the Southern Baptist Convention, plagiarized significant portions of a 2020 sermon he gave at Redemption Church—the church he pastors—in Mobile, Alabama, from a sermon

J. D. Greear had given to his church in 2019.[2] Further investigation revealed even more uncited use of others' material in Litton's sermons. The incident sparked a widespread debate in the SBC and in wider evangelicalism over sermon plagiarism, even leading at least one state Baptist convention to adopt a resolution condemning the practice.[3] For his part, Greear defended Litton and said he'd granted permission for his material's use, credited or uncredited, and many evangelical pastors jumped to defend the practice generally.

Josh Howerton, lead pastor of megachurch Lakepointe Church in Dallas, Texas—himself a figure with many relational and public connections to those in the gospel-centered tribe—provided a widely read defense of sermon plagiarism, writing,

> A church-sermon is not an academia-dissertation or a book/journalism-publication. I freely give away my notes to other pastors, because pastors aren't preaching to make themselves look good, sound smart, or sell something proprietary. We're preaching for life-change and to grow the kingdom. Those differing goals of written communication in journalism or academia vs. the goals of verbal communication in preaching lead to very different standards. Frankly, this is why "sermon plagiarism"

---

2. Bob Smietana, "New SBC President Ed Litton Apologizes for Using JD Greear Sermon Quotes without Credit," *Religion News*, June 26, 2021, https://religion news.com/2021/06/26/new-sbc-president-ed-litton-apologizes-for-using-j-d-greear -sermon-quotes-without-credit-god-whisper-homosexuality-sin-romans/.

3. Liam Adams, "Tennessee Southern Baptists Condemn Plagiarism in a Critique of New SBC President," *The Tennessean*, November 18, 2021, https://www .tennessean.com/story/news/religion/2021/11/18/tennessee-baptists-plagiarism -resolution-debate-sbc-president/8654413002/.

accusations almost never come from other pastors, but from journalists, writers, or academics (or professional pastor-critics who need to manufacture new "scandals" to generate clicks for their monetized sites), trying to impose the standards of their industry onto another field.[4]

Howerton marshals the support of figures from church history like Charles Spurgeon and Martin Luther, as well as some from more recent history like John Maxwell and T. D. Jakes, to make his case, which is not just flippant and flimsy, but a fundamental category error of what a sermon *is*. He may be rightly distinguishing preaching from an academic journal entry or book manuscript, but he is still treating it as a consumer good, interchangeable from church to church, a product that may be replicated ad infinitum for the download of any religious customers one happens to find himself in front of.

Contrary to Howerton's and many others' protests, it's not difficult to give credit in oral communication. Plagiarism is dishonest, and over time it undermines a congregation's trust that their preacher is biblically qualified to shepherd. Scripturally speaking, "able to teach" (1 Tim. 3:2) does not simply mean "able to speak well"; it means able to rightly divide (2 Tim. 2:15), competently exegete, and faithfully contextualize God's Word to one's flock. If a preacher is merely regurgitating someone else's "ability to teach," how can we be confident in his qualification?

Further, the preacher who plagiarizes his sermons and otherwise treats his preaching and teaching as marketable

---

4. Josh Howerton, "On 'Sermon Plagiarism' Accusations," JoshHowerton.com, September 9, 2022, https://joshhowerton.com/2022/09/09/on-sermon-plagiarism/.

products reflects a superficial understanding of the spiritual work of ministry, which is not a franchising of the faith but a contextual rootedness of a church nourished by the spiritual rootedness of her pastors.

The reframing of church resources as culturally relevant content creation is just another sign of evangelical superficiality, and it has made distressing inroads among a fractured gospel-centered movement whose individual organizations and networks are all vying for superior market share.

## Spiritually Arrested Development

Thomas Bergler traces the historic roots of American evangelicalism's cultural relevance idol to the emergence of the cultural concept of the "teenager." As the wider world latched onto a new consumer demographic, so did the church. Bergler describes teen-targeted church ministries in the 1940s:

> Young people, many of whom had never seen old-time religion anywhere but in church, found it exciting to attend rallies in theaters, civic auditoriums, and even stadiums. In the age before television, participating in a live radio broadcast was a thrilling media event. An army of traveling evangelists and musicians made Youth for Christ rallies their full time work. Many teenagers also got the chance to become Christian "stars." Local rally directors recruited and trained teenage musical acts that performed old gospel music favorites in contemporary music styles; at a rally in Kansas City in 1947, a trio sang "I Have a Great Salvation"

in the style of the popular Boswell Sisters. Indeed, the music at YFC meetings was close enough to the crooner, girl trio, and big band styles of the day to arouse the ire of some fundamentalists and the scorn of mainline Protestants. But teenagers loved it.[5]

It is not difficult to trace a line from these culturally adapted youth rallies in the mid-twentieth century to the "God at the Movies" sermon series in the twenty-first. The teenagers never really grew up.

In the late 1970s to the mid-1980s, young Baby Boomers were asking (legitimate) questions about the helpfulness of the dominant church culture in winning lost people to Jesus. Their conclusions, while mostly sincere, resulted in the rise of the "seeker church," churches that attempted to refract Christianity through the language of the culture in order to demonstrate the faith's cultural relevance. However, this long experiment has largely proved a methodological failure[6] and spiritual failure.[7] But the experiment continues, and the result has been a decades-long youth group rally for American evangelicalism.

How did the attractional paradigm become the dominant mode of church ministry in American life? Why do so many evangelical church services include extraneous production

---

5. Bergler, *Juvenilization*, 50.

6. I've included data demonstrating this previously in Jared C. Wilson, *The Prodigal Church: A Gentle Manifesto against the Status Quo* (Wheaton, IL: Crossway, 2015).

7. See a further development of this argument in Jared C. Wilson, *The Gospel-Driven Church: Uniting Church Growth Dreams with the Metrics of Grace* (Grand Rapids: Zondervan, 2019).

elements more befitting stage shows and rock concerts? Why are more and more churches resorting to silly gimmicks and over-the-top theatrics to attract crowds? This is the extension of a youth group mentality into the gathered worship of the wider church. Think of it as the "dumbing up" of American churches.

But one thing I have noted over my thirty years in church ministry is not just youth group creeping into the church body but youth group declining in the quality and theological content of their preaching and teaching. In the early days of working in student ministry, we used food, games, and music to get students in the door so they could hear a biblical message. Increasingly these days, the food, games, and music are becoming the message. The teaching itself becomes merely a feature of equal weight among the bells and whistles.

I do sense there is a concerted effort by Gen-Z and Millennial leaders to turn back the tide of juvenilization in the church started by their Boomer and Gen-X forebears. But the prevailing messaging in a ministry dedicated to cultural relevance is overly shaped by the culture it's trying to reach. When it's not entertainment-minded pop inspiration, it's gauzy therapy-speak, "authentic" teaching with the appearance of depth but full of buzzwords and catchphrases aimed at emotional reaction rather than spiritual devotion. And as our culture is superficial, so too becomes our teaching.

I was speaking at a pastors' conference recently and presented a basic exposition of Scripture in my exhortation to the leaders present to focus their ministry on the glory of Jesus. Afterward, more than one attendee thanked me for, in the words of one, "actually using the Bible" in my talk. We should not take for granted that at explicitly Christian events targeted at Christian leaders we will hear an explicitly Christian message. These days we certainly should not take it for granted that we would hear such a thing at a Christian church!

Stephen Nichols writes, "The commodification of Christianity not only exploits and subjects the faith to the cultural form of consumer capitalism, but it also sentimentalizes and trivializes faith."[8]

This trivialized version of the faith is epidemic in evangelicalism. It is the reason our church services feel shallow. It is the reason our public faith is so brittle.

In the words of J. T. English,

> I believe it is time for the church to ask some serious questions about our shared disease and how we can begin to create depth that might lead to breadth. Perhaps the church should start thinking about what it means to go deeper with fewer instead of going wider with the many. What if our cultural moment is inviting the church to embody the depth and substance of the Christian faith, not a shallow spirituality that appeals to the masses?[9]

We often drift from gospel-centrality because we do not see how versatile, how resilient, how *big* the gospel really is. The Bible speaks of the news of Christ's finished work as

---

8. Stephen J. Nichols, *Jesus Made in America: A Cultural History from the Puritans to* The Passion of the Christ (Downers Grove, IL: InterVarsity Press, 2008), 196.

9. J. T. English, *Deep Discipleship: How the Church Can Make Whole Disciples of Jesus* (Nashville: B&H, 2020), 9.

more than just the grounds of our justification, but also as the power for our sanctification and the assurance of our glorification. When we have a less than deep understanding of the gospel, we will be tempted to look for our depth elsewhere. But the gospel is deeper than we often realize.

How do we break free from spiritual arrested development? Some will say it is important to move beyond the ABCs of the gospel. But what if an inattention to the "first importance" (1 Cor. 15:3) of the good news is exactly what's keeping us so immature?

## Gospel Deeps

All of the indulgence in and employment of superficiality in our ministry is based on a distrust of the gospel to captivate. We do not think the gospel will "do the trick." We must dress it up and make it fancy.

Some, rather ironically, see the gospel as merely an introductory thing, the shallow end of the Christian pool, and thus itself too superficial for routine fixation.

Is it? Do we "move on" from the gospel?

Some have claimed the Bible teaches us to do so. One common prooftext for the claim is Hebrews 6:1–2:

> Therefore let us leave the elementary doctrine of Christ and go on to maturity, not laying again a foundation of repentance from dead works and of faith toward God, and of instruction about washings, the laying on of hands, the resurrection of the dead, and eternal judgment.

Is the author of Hebrews telling us to move on from elementary *gospel* truths?[10]

This may seem like an odd question, but it is one I get occasionally whenever I stump hard for constantly returning to the centrality of Christ's finished work for both the lost *and the found.* I remember several years ago a prominent evangelical scholar citing this passage in his criticism of my work on this point. A few years ago I was reminded again by an online critic of the alleged "graduation" from the gospel encouraged by Hebrews 6.

Yet the apostle Paul tells us in the opening verses of 1 Corinthians 15 that the gospel is of first importance. As I argued in chapter 1, I don't believe Paul means *initial* importance but *primary* (central) importance. This is why he's "reminding" the Corinthians about it. Over and over again, Paul instructs his readers to only hold true to what they've already attained (Phil. 3:16), to lay hold of what has laid hold of them (Phil. 3:12), and so forth. So I don't believe the author of Hebrews is telling us in Hebrews 6 that we graduate from the gospel to other things.

So to what does the text refer?

It's a complex passage, but as with every text, the context helps. In Hebrews 5:12 we read, "In fact, though by this time you ought to be teachers, you need someone to teach you the elementary truths of God's Word all over again" (NIV). The dilemma is seeing how the recipients of the letter would need

---

10. A portion of the following paragraphs originally appeared in Jared C. Wilson, "Does Hebrews 6 Teach That We Should Move On from the Gospel?" The Gospel Coalition, March 14, 2019, https://www.thegospelcoalition.org/article/hebrews-6-teach-move-gospel/.

to both relearn the elementary principles of the oracles of God and leave the elementary teachings about Christ (6:1–2). Unless the author is speaking out of both sides of his mouth, these must mean two different things.

I believe the "elementary teachings" in Hebrews 6 refer to the types and shadows of the old covenant, about which Hebrews says quite a bit (e.g., 8:5; 10:1; see also Col. 2:17). So the exhortation here is not about leaving the gospel behind but about leaving the shadows behind to walk in the light of Christ. And further, the admonition is to grow up in the gospel beyond initial repentance and individual salvation. It's about following the signposts into the land of destination. It's a call to maturity that is gospel-driven, not post-gospel or even gospel-latent.

John Calvin concurs, writing of this passage,

[H]e bids them to leave these rudiments, not that the faithful are ever to forget them, but that they are not to remain in them; and this idea appears more clear from what follows, the comparison of a *foundation*; for in building a house we must never leave the foundation; and yet to be always engaged in laying it, would be ridiculous. For as the foundation is laid for the sake of what is built on it, he who is occupied in laying it and proceeds not to the superstruction, wearies himself with foolish and useless labour.[11]

In any event, I don't believe Hebrews 6 means the gospel is the ABCs and now we need to buckle down and learn the

---

11. John Calvin, *Commentaries on the Epistle of Paul the Apostle to the Hebrews*, Calvin's Commentaries 22 (Grand Rapids: Baker, 2009), 131.

hard stuff. The ABCs of salvation are the rudiments of the "advanced linguistics" of the gospel deeps. You build on top of a foundation that remains, and no matter how high and big you build your house, you never leave the foundation, or you'll experience some serious structural weakness.

Indeed, if the gospel is so resilient that it powers not only our conversion but also our sanctification (1 Cor. 15:2; 2 Cor. 3:18; Titus 2:11–12), it would be foolish to "move on" from it. As Tim Keller argues, "The gospel is a clear and present word, but it is not a simplistic word."[12] In fact, the gospel is itself the deepest subject given to us. First Peter 1:12 tells us that "angels long to look" into the good news. If the grace of Christ is a resource deep enough to sustain angelic fascination, how pitiful our fog machines and therapeutic homilies must look to them. How superficial our incessant dawdling into the graceless practicalities of application must be.

Evangelicals drift into superficiality when they find the gospel elementary, simplistic, or boring. We delude ourselves into thinking we are forging out into deeper levels of the faith, when in fact we have unhitched ourselves from the deepest well and strongest power available to us.

In the good news, we find the message of forgiveness, the promise of imputed righteousness, and the hope of future glorification. In the good news, we see the glory of Christ's substitutionary atonement, his cosmic triumph over the powers of evil, and his conquest of death and hell. In the good news, we discover divine power for getting through the day, getting through our lives, and getting through the grave. This

---

12. Timothy Keller, *Center Church: Doing Balanced, Gospel-Centered Ministry in Your City* (Grand Rapids: Zondervan, 2012), 39.

is not basic stuff. It is simple enough a child can understand and believe, yet it is deep enough to keep us spiritually challenged for all eternity.

To center on the gospel, then, is to repent of spiritual superficiality. To center on the gospel is to protect ourselves from drifting into thinking we know better than the God who saved us. To center on the gospel is certainly to immerse ourselves in the depths of glorious grace. It is the gospel that roots and grounds us in love so we "may have strength to comprehend with all the saints what is the breadth and length and height and depth, and to know the love of Christ that surpasses knowledge" (Eph. 3:18–19).

Keller again: "Because the gospel is endlessly rich, it can handle the burden of being the one 'main thing' of a church."[13]

---

13. Keller, *Center Church*, 36.

Chapter Six

# Less than Powerful

## A Drift into Pragmatism

*Watch out; beware of . . .*
*the leaven of Herod.*
**—Mark 8:15**

AFTER THE COLLAPSE OF MARS HILL CHURCH IN SEATTLE,
Mark Driscoll laid low for about five minutes. Then he re-
appeared in Arizona, poised to plant a new church. And along
with the new church came a new persona. Where Driscoll had
previously built a significant platform among the "young,
restless, and Reformed" tribe by unapologetically espous-
ing a Reformed soteriology, he now said, "I don't hold to
the five points of Calvinism. I think it's garbage."[1] Where
he'd previously spent a lot of decibels and spilled a lot of ink
arguing for a strict complementarian view of manhood and
womanhood, he now cooperated with egalitarian conference
leaders and placed his wife's name alongside his own at the top
of his church plant's leadership org chart. Where he'd once
vociferously criticized the kind of attractional ministries that
downplay theology and play up a kind of prosperity gospel,
he now found in such churches valuable allies in the attempt
to rehabilitate his image. No longer the angry young prophet,
Driscoll positioned himself as a kindly spiritual father.[2] It was
quite the about-face.

Some admirers of Driscoll were left confused by this apparent reinvention. Did he really no longer believe the theology
and ministry philosophy he had used to build Mars Hill and
to extend his reach from it? Did he ever really believe them?

1. "Real Conversations: Pastor Mark Driscoll, Part 2," *The Debrief Podcast
with Matthew Stephen Brown*, June 4, 2019, YouTube video, 1:07:25, https://www
.youtube.com/watch?v=4OsQm6YU3OY&t=3520s.
2. Kevin Porter, "Mark Driscoll Tells Perry Noble He's Learning to Be
'Spiritual Father,'" *Christian Post*, March 17, 2016, https://www.christianpost.com
/news/mark-driscoll-perry-noble-spiritual-father-newspring-conference.html.

This reinvention was the artistry of a pragmatist at work. As mentioned in the introduction, this work had begun before his "fall" and the closing of Mars Hill, as he began to more self-consciously depict himself as a "spiritual father," a kinder, gentler version of his firebrand self.[3] Driscoll is a gifted showman and salesman. As a theologian, he is somewhat of a chameleon, able to blend into whatever cultural stance or leadership persona he feels is most advantageous to attract the consumer demographic he most desires at the time. In the last few years, his persona has shifted even more, reconnecting with his formerly macho personality and employing a lot of the language of "anti-wokeness" and the "alpha male" manosphere. Despite all of his bluster about convictions and courage, Driscoll is a man with his finger in the wind.

This realization was quite jarring for me personally. When I was waking up to the spiritual bankruptcy of the pragmatism in the attractional church, Driscoll's voice was one of the first I'd heard that offered a refuge into gospel-centrality. He rejected the superficiality of the seeker church, preached expositionally, and believed in the ongoing operation of the Holy Spirit's power. Further, he claimed to be a "charismatic with a seat belt."[4] As a continuationist, I found such a claim especially intriguing. He gave all the indications of rejecting what I was rejecting and affirming what I was affirming. Yet when I noticed him flirting with the attractional ministry philosophy he'd so often critiqued, I began to realize just

3. Drew Dyck, "The Survivor," *Leadership Journal*, Winter 2014, 37–39.
4. Mark Driscoll, "Tough Text Thursday: 1 Corinthians 13," Pastor Mark Driscoll online, December 15, 2011, https://archive.ph/20140502041439/http://pastormark.tv/2011/12/15/tough-text-thursday-1-corinthians-13.

how insidious the spirit of pragmatism is. And over the last ten years, I've watched it weave and wind its way through the teaching and practice of many ostensibly "gospel-centered" ministries.

Mark Dever has said, "The greatest threat to the gospel specific to today is the indirect challenge of pragmatism among evangelicals."[5] And further, I think that perhaps the most *multifaceted* danger facing evangelicalism today is a pragmatism that taints everything with which it comes into contact.

The church loses sight of the gospel when we trade in its spiritual power for programs, formulas, and strategies we trust more readily for results. We can see this in our churches, and we can see it in the way evangelicals think about missions and their place generally in the wider culture. We trust politics, protests, and pontificating to do what only the Holy Spirit speaking through the good news can do. But we embrace pragmatism under the banner of "gospel-centrality" when we act like the gospel is not powerful enough to meet our aims.

## More than One Kind of Worldliness

In Mark 8 we find Jesus and his disciples in a boat after a long day of ministry. Earlier, Jesus performed another

---

5. This line originally appeared in a blog post by Mark Dever published on the Together 4 the Gospel website, which is no longer active. However, this line also appears in a different online article: "The Great Threat to the Gospel Today," *Poikilos*, March 31, 2006, https://wmson.wordpress.com/2006/03/31/the-great -threat-to-the-gospel-today/.

miracle, providing food for a crowd of four thousand people. Afterward, he is accosted by a group of religious leaders who demand he perform another miracle. Between hungry crowds and demanding factions, I imagine our Lord is tired. But he still takes the opportunity to teach his friends a lesson derived from the day's encounters.

"Watch out," he says to the disciples; "beware of the leaven of the Pharisees and the leaven of Herod" (Mark 8:15). (Some manuscripts on the latter part read "the Herodians," rather than Herod proper.)

The concept of leaven throughout the Scriptures works as a metaphorical reference to something that is growing, spreading, or expanding. Some teachers have argued that leaven in the Bible always refers to the gangrenous influence of sin, but this seems patently false, given that Jesus also compares the kingdom of heaven to leaven (Matt. 13:33). Nevertheless, in this instance, which is a warning, Jesus is clearly telling the disciples to stay alert about the possible influence of the Pharisees and Herodians.

We know from Luke 23:8 that Herod has expected a sign from Jesus. Perhaps Jesus is referring to the desire, from both the Pharisees and Herod, for religious entertainment and the desire to use Jesus for their own ends. (This is the inherent danger in all of the miracles Jesus performs: that the witnesses would come to love the miracles more than Christ himself.) But I think there is something else at play here, something in the distinction between "of the Pharisees" and "of Herod." Two kinds of leaven are being warned about here, two categories of evil influence.

We find further corroboration of this perspective in the

parallel account in Matthew 16:6, where Jesus says to the disciples, "Watch and beware of the leaven of the Pharisees and *Sadducees*" (emphasis added). All of these representative groups may look to use Jesus for their own ends (seeking a sign), but they still represent different ideologies and cultures. I'm convinced the pharisaical leaven corresponds to a kind of Christless religiosity, which is what we might today call "legalism" (though certainly some nuance is needed in our discussion of what constitutes legalism, which I hope to introduce in the next chapter). The leaven of Herod and the Sadducees, then, corresponds to a kind of worldliness. The Sadducees, remember, are a Jewish sect who have become theologically and culturally compromised. Unlike the Pharisees, who still held firmly to the Hebrew Scriptures, the Sadducees denied a future bodily resurrection and other spiritually vital teachings of the law. They also occupied the place of cultural elitism, collaborating with the Roman occupiers in a bid for their own power and privilege.

This is a bit of a crass analogy, but the Pharisees of Jesus' day would be like the conservatives of our day and the Sadducees would be more like the liberals. The comparisons don't line up perfectly, but we can certainly see the connections between the two categories.

When Jesus warns about the leaven of Herod and the leaven of the Sadducees, he's warning about the influence of fleshly interest in our thinking and living. (As the Sadducees represent religious conformity to the secular, Herod represents the nakedly secular—the pagan power that holds the allure. If the Sadducees are compromised by worldliness, Herod is worldliness personified.) Apart from the direct threat of explicit heresy or willful disobedience to God's commands, I cannot think of a more worldly threat to evangelicals than pragmatism.

Mind you, worldliness doesn't always look like wanton hedonism. When Christians hear the word *worldly*, we often immediately think of things like sexual immorality, drunkenness, or overt greed and covetousness. But there's more than one kind of worldliness. Worldliness is simply being influenced or directed by the spirit of the world, which is in opposition to the Spirit of Christ. Worldliness is being shaped by the values of what is passing away, rather than the values of the eternal kingdom.

Pragmatism is a kind of worldliness because it trades reliance on the Holy Spirit—and the wisdom of the words he has inspired—for the strength of the flesh. Pragmatism is worldliness because it walks by sight, not faith. "Wherever pragmatism exists in the church," Daniel Dickard writes, "there is always a corresponding deemphasis of Christ's sufficiency, God's sovereignty, biblical integrity, the power of prayer, and Spirit-led ministries."[6]

Evangelicals embody the spirit of the world whenever they disengage from prayer. Evangelicals embody the spirit of the world whenever they marginalize the gospel in favor of something else they assume is better suited for its job. These are just some of the fruits of pragmatism, where formulas, strategies, and results are trusted as more reliable than word and spirit.

The overarching premise of gospel-centrality is that the

---

6. Daniel C. Dickard, *Church Together: The Church of We in the Age of Me* (Eugene, OR: Wipf and Stock, 2022), 55.

gospel really can bear the weight of being the "operating system" of the Christian life and church. But we see the leaven of Herod begin to spread when we become selective about what the gospel applies to . . . and what it doesn't.

## Gospel-Centrism, Not Gospel-Onlyism[7]

One giant tell of a believer's personal biases (and cultural anxieties) is to look at which issues they think can be solved by "just preaching the gospel" and which they think will not be solved by such a remedy. Like a slow-motion car crash, I have witnessed over the last ten years some of the loudest evangelical voices online insist that the problem of racism (if they think such a problem even exists) is a "sin problem, not a skin problem," and thus solvable simply by preaching the gospel. Yet these same voices also insist that just preaching the gospel is not enough to address the onslaught of moral chaos in our culture brought on by the LGBTQ+ agenda. It is fascinating to see, according to some Christians, which powers the gospel is suited for and which it is not.

Many once happily gospel-centered Christians have moved on from the philosophy because they found it not robust enough for the cultural and spiritual challenges of our post-Christian twenty-first-century world. Those heavily invested in the issues related to men, women, and sexuality

---

7. Portions of the following section originally appeared in Jared C. Wilson, "The Perils of Preaching an Implications-Free Gospel," For the Church, August 28, 2018, https://ftc.co/resource-library/blog-entries/the-perils-of-preaching-an-implications-free-gospel/.

argue that gospel-centrality did not prepare young people for how to be biblical men and women in an age of gender confusion. Social justice advocates argue that gospel-centrality did not give them the philosophical equipment required for missional praxis beyond the theoretical. Those invested in race conversations argue that gospel-centrality does not go deep enough to help us address either systemic issues in our nation and culture or practical issues related to partiality or even "reverse racism" in our communities and churches.

I know this will seem like sleight of hand to many critics, but the truth is that I believe many of those who have moved on from gospel-centrality to teaching and philosophy they find more effective never really understood gospel-centrality in principle. They did not know the substance of the philosophy. They only knew the cultural expression of it, the tribal identity of it. They attended "gospel-centered" churches and went to "gospel-centered" conferences and fellowshipped with other "gospel-centered" believers, but none of it equipped them for the coming storms because their gospel-centrality was merely a cultural overlay to the pragmatism that has been for decades a matter of evangelical course.

Those of us who promote gospel-centrality need to say clearly that we are not gospel-*onlyists*. We are gospel-*centrists*.

To put the gospel at the center of our life and ministry is not to erase the practicalities of the Christian faith and the gospel's implications. Being practical and embracing pragmatism are not the same thing. The Bible is eminently practical. But the Bible's practicalities emerge from a centered gospel. The finished work of Christ is freighted with implications. Thus, while the gospel is indeed the skeleton key for any challenge or sin we will face, "just preach the gospel" is actually never really the right answer to these challenges and sins. The gospel is indeed not its implications. And yet—and yet!—to preach an implications-free gospel is in essence to strip Christ's lordship from his salvation. "Just preach the gospel" is not the full counsel of God's Word.

First of all, the gospel does not exist in a theological vacuum. The ministry of Jesus Christ that saves us had a cultural and missiological context. The Scriptures that for thousands of years testified to him are a substantive foundation for understanding all of his works, both teaching and doing, in the four Gospels. And the extrapolation of his atoning work by the apostles in the rest of the New Testament represents an important "and then what?"—for both our thinking and our doing—that the Holy Spirit determined we should feed on as God's very words.

We need only look at the substantive testimony of the prophets to Israel and to the kings and nations in the Old Testament to see how much time is spent specifically rebuking and calling to repentance the powers that be in order to see that the precedent is biblical.

Jesus' longest sermon (Matt. 5–7) and one of his longest parables (Luke 10:25–37) are almost entirely about love of neighbor in the face of cultural-religious opposition and systemic injustice and corruption. All of that is to say, Jesus did not come preaching the gospel simply *as idea* but rather *as kingdom.*

Further, the Bible commands obedience! This is a most facile point, I know, and one that should be the most unnecessary, but: Does the Bible actually outline implications of the gospel? Are the moral imperatives of Scripture binding on Christians? Is the whole of Scripture sufficient for reproof, correction, and training in righteousness (2 Tim. 3:16)? Is faith proved by its works (James 2:17–18)?

If the answer to all of those questions is yes, then even as we hold the central message distinct from its entailments, we nevertheless have no right to disconnect them.

Gospel-centrality is not gospel-onlyism; thus, gospel-centrality is not antinomianism.

This does not mean, however, that the imperatives can do what the indicatives can do. It doesn't mean the law has any power of its own to give us on its behalf. That power can only come from the gospel. Yet the one true gospel empowers its implications. We are created for good works. It is good and right and biblical to teach that.

Furthermore, the gospel is adorned and amplified by its implications. If the Lord wanted us to have an unadorned gospel, we would not need Romans 12–16; 1 Corinthians 3–16; 2 Corinthians 5–13; the second halves of Galatians, Ephesians, and Colossians; and so on. What I mean is, if the gospel is not simply central but isolatable, we can lop off huge portions of the New Testament, not to mention gigantic swaths of the Old.

Do you want to go back to the "ask Jesus into your heart" gospel? Because that's where the implications-free teaching goes. To fail to urge obedience to the gospel (1 Peter 4:17) is to rob Scripture of riches, the gospel of raiment, and God of glory. In Galatians 2, as Paul is recounting getting on the same page with the apostles before him, he mentions that a prevailing concern on his mission was that he remember the poor. Why?

Because while the imperatives aren't the message that saves, they are nevertheless imperative to the mission to save!

I know within the larger conversation there are hundreds of smaller, more specific subjects to address. Many critics of social justice advocacy do not say we should avoid teaching imperatives. (They either simply don't think the problems of social justice are real or don't believe that the particular imperatives proposed are the right ones.) But many folks do appear to be saying we ought to avoid imperatives. I see it from influential teachers and Jane and Joe Pew-sitters alike. Some do say or suggest we ought to just preach the gospel. And while it seems sound and even seems "gospel-centered," it forgets that the gospel, if it's real, has a multitude of implications that follow in the wake of our belief.

Finally, if we do not apply the gospel's implications biblically, we leave it to others to do so heretically. Perhaps you've seen the provocative and tragic photo from history of the Ku Klux Klansmen standing beneath a banner that declares "Jesus Saves." The sobering truth is that many of our religious forefathers and theological heroes made tremendous compromises with worldliness as a result of poor application or no application of the gospel to cultural ills and systemic injustices.

"Just preaching the gospel" did not appear to cure much of the racism enmeshed within a very Protestant white culture in the historic American South. (The photo in question actually comes from Portland, Oregon, interestingly enough.) Why do we suspect we are any more spiritually evolved than they? We look up to them so much, yet we suspect we need less exhortation than they.

I do not believe the vast majority of those who criticize the so-called social justice movement do so out of racial animus. Yet if we do not teach the full counsel of God's Word and hold people specifically accountable to it, we give false assurances and enable all manner of hard-heartedness. Many of these critics lead or covenant in churches that practice biblical church discipline of unrepentant members. In such cases, they realize "just preach the gospel" is not sufficient; the gospel must be applied biblically, or it can be taken for granted by some that it does not speak to specific areas of their lives.

I know the objection will be made that nobody really believes we shouldn't help people apply the gospel to the obedience that proves they believe it. But the way so many do this only for selective areas of concern leads me to think we are more okay with some sins than others. Typically we are less okay with the sins of others and more lenient with any exhortation to repentance that indicts ourselves.

The gospel selectively applied constitutes hypocrisy.

I think of the way so many in my Reformed tribe have dutifully cultivated a reputation for quarrelsomeness and judgmentalism. We are a people who have staked our doctrinal identity on *grace*, and yet we seem to have a lot of trouble offering that grace to others. It is telling how much such staunch defenders of the gospel seem to prefer the leverage of the law.

This kind of hypocrisy is rampant on social media and in our own relational circles. We assume "just the gospel" is enough for us, while long and prolonged deconstructions, critiques, "take-downs," and refutations are exactly what's needed for others. It is textbook plank-speck type stuff (Matt. 7:3–5).

What's the solution? Well, it's the gospel! The gospel is the cure for sin. The gospel alone has power to justify, heal, and reconcile us. But the gospel that alone saves does not come alone. And indeed, if we cannot help each other see where we are "not in step with the truth of the gospel" (Gal. 2:14), we deny that very power, and in effect deny that very gospel.

The gospel is indeed the antidote to every sin and suffering. But "just preach the gospel" misses the mark as the solution to all manner of ills, because the good news has necessary implications that adorn and amplify it.

Nevertheless, when we center the implications, and thereby marginalize the gospel, we show the leaven of Herod and the Sadducees. We show our pragmatic thinking, which puts us wading farther and farther away from the spiritual renewal needed in our lives and in our world.

## Quenching the Spirit

We must remember that the Christian life is not fundamentally about a set of behaviors, but a set of characteristics. Pragmatism doesn't get us that. Only walking with the Spirit does.

Note in Galatians 5:19–23 that when the apostle Paul cautions against "the works of the flesh," he lists mainly sinful things we *do*. But when he contrasts these with "the fruit of the Spirit," he lists mainly things we *are*.

This does not mean that moral and religious behavior is unnecessary; it is only that the behavior that truly honors

God emerges from a heart that truly honors God. And to have a heart that truly honors God, operating on the surface of the pragmatic will not suffice. Remember the second principle of gospel-centrality: People change by grace, not law. Only the Holy Spirit working through the gospel can go deep enough to effect real heart change.

Here is an imperative the gospel empowers us to obey: "Do not quench the Spirit" (1 Thess. 5:19). When our Christianity is run through with pragmatism, our Christian lives may feel more accomplished and manageable, our churches may get bigger and run like well-oiled machines, but we are saying to the Holy Spirit, "We don't really need you. We've got it figured out."

Taking a step back and looking at the evangelical landscape, is there really any doubt that the spirit of pragmatism has had catastrophic effects? Our churches operate as factories of vague "God-talk" where attendees go to get their weekly pick-me-ups. Our church members feel increasingly adrift in a world of moral chaos and oppressive idolatries, with no real biblical anchors given to them. Is it any wonder they chase after the latest inspirational gobbledygook to get through the day or the most self-assured public officials to be their political messiahs?

Is there really any doubt that we need more of God's Spirit?

In 1 Thessalonians 1:5–6, Paul praises the church's resemblance to Christ and the pattern of apostolic witness to Christ, saying this has come about "because our gospel came to you not only in word, but also in power and in the Holy Spirit and with full conviction."

At the place of hardship, challenge, or defeat, we need less of our own know-how and more of God's Word.

But even the way we use the Bible can still be permeated with pragmatism. Warning about some subtle ways professing Christians may abandon the authority of the Bible, D. A. Carson writes thusly about American pragmatism:

One form of this approach to texts, often dubbed American pragmatism, thinks of readers as "users" of the text. A "good" reading, for example, is one that meets specific needs in the reader or the community. There is much to be said in favor of this stance, but it becomes self-defeating when it says, in effect, that a "good" reading meets particular needs on the part of the reader or community and must not be thought of as conveying timeless truth. . . . . American pragmatism defends itself with an ostensible timeless truth about the virtues of American pragmatism. Pretty soon the commentaries that work out of this tradition do not so much help us think about God and his character and work, as about what we think we need and how the biblical texts meet those needs. The door is opened to interpretations that are exploitative, merely current, sometimes cutesy, and invariably agenda driven, but only accidentally grounded in responsible exegesis.[8]

I cannot help but think of the countless "felt need" sermons my first ministry training directed me to preach—sermons that used the Bible but did not actually preach it.

8. D. A. Carson, *The Gospel and the Modern World: A Theological Vision for the Church*, ed. Brian J. Tabb (Wheaton, IL: Crossway, 2023), 135.

I cannot help but think of voices today like Andy Stanley, who discourages teaching phrases like "The Bible says so."[9]

The reason Stanley is wrong to discourage such usage is because God is real and his Word is powerful, and neither needs our help or apology.

The profound irony of pragmatism in Christianity is that it promises to more completely concretize our faith while it simultaneously marginalizes *the object* of our faith!

One hundred years ago, J. Gresham Machen warned us about the threat of pragmatism to our functional theology:

> Certainly no part of Jesus' knowledge of God was merely theoretical; everything that Jesus knew about God touched His heart and determined His actions. In that sense, Jesus' knowledge of God was "practical." But unfortunately that is not the sense in which the assertion of modern liberalism is meant. What is frequently meant by a "practical" knowledge of God in modern parlance is not a theoretical knowledge of God that is also practical, but a practical knowledge which is not theoretical—in other words, a knowledge which gives no information about objective reality, a knowledge which is no knowledge at all. And nothing could possibly be more unlike the religion of Jesus than that.[10]

What is truly needed, then, is not more "practical application." It is not more religious or cultural strategies for

---

9. Andy Stanley with Thomas Horrocks, "Andy Stanley: Why 'The Bible Says So' Is Not Enough Anymore," *Outreach Magazine*, May 20, 2018, https://outreachmagazine.com/features/19900-the-bible-says-so.html.

10. J. Gresham Machen, *Christianity and Liberalism* (Sanford, FL: Ligonier, 2023), 53–54.

"winning." What is needed is a waving of the white flag of surrender and more openhearted devotion to the "one little word" that makes even the devil tremble. If we will see a work of revival—and of reformation—in our day, it will begin with a desperate return to the power of the gospel of Jesus Christ as the most important news in all the universe.

Richard Lovelace once wrote, "It is not merely new methods, new insights and clearer theologies which will advance the gospel at the close of the twentieth century. It must be a cleansing of man's spirit, and therefore a pouring out of the Holy Spirit of God."[11]

The gospel primarily confers to us not a set of ideas, but a *person*—the person of Jesus Christ. Drifting into pragmatism—even in our avowed gospel interest!—quenches the spirit of Christ's influence in our lives. The need, then, is to resituate ourselves in the crosshairs of the Holy Spirit, which, biblically speaking, means paying closer attention to the gospel lest we drift away from it.

## Gospel-Centrality as a Pathway to Spiritual Renewal

As it applies to the Christian life and Christian ministry, pragmatism is anti-spiritual. It is anti-spiritual because it centers on the power of human ingenuity and technique. We can be pragmatic, or we can rely on the Holy Spirit, but we can't do both.

---

11. Richard Lovelace, *Dynamics of Spiritual Life: An Evangelical Theology of Renewal* (Downers Grove, IL: InterVarsity Press, 1979), 200.

In chapter 8 we will more thoroughly survey the key ways Christians center on the gospel, but the present concern of pragmatism calls for a review of some others. We can begin by rehearsing the three principles of gospel-centrality:

1. The whole Bible is about Jesus.
2. People change by grace, not law.
3. Our ultimate validation is found not in our performance, but in Christ's.

I am convinced that a recommitment to these truths of historic Reformational Christianity will begin our pathway to spiritual renewal. I am also convinced that a commitment to these truths will prove the remedy to the leaven of Herod and the Sadducees.

How so?

Let us turn each principle into a series of diagnostic questions—to ourselves and to our personal worlds. The answers can help out the spirit of pragmatism in our lives. The answers will tell us whether we are trusting more in the flesh or in God's Spirit.

### The whole Bible is about Jesus.

- When I read the Bible, am I more interested in the information I'm learning than in the person I'm becoming?
- When I read the Bible, do I more readily see how it ought to convict others than how it ought to convict me?
- When I read the Bible, am I mostly using it to win arguments or to win people?

- When I read the Bible, am I looking more for affirmation of my secondary or tertiary doctrinal views than I am looking for the glory of Jesus?
- When I read the Bible, do I get more excited about good works than I do the good news?
- In my preaching and teaching, is Christ or the Christian the star of the show?

## People change by grace, not law.

- Am I more self-conscious about holy behavior than I am holy character?
- Do I feel the itch to add a "yes, but" whenever someone emphasizes the good news over good works?
- Would my loved ones say they are clearer on my expectations of them than on my acceptance of them?
- Do I more readily correct than encourage?
- In my preaching and teaching, do I emphasize practical application over the finished work of Christ?

## Our ultimate validation is found not in our performance, but in Christ's.

- At the end of the day, do I find my rest more easily in my accomplishments than in Christ's love?
- Do I feel ruled by my awareness of my deficiencies and failures?
- Do I feel justified by my appraisal of my successes?
- Do I think I'm only as good as what I've done (or haven't done)?

- Do I tend to make excuses for unethical or immoral persons—including myself—so long as they "get the job done"?
- In my ministry, do I consider visible growth metrics as the main justification of methods?

Answers to these questions don't tell us everything, and certainly there are more that we could ask to probe deeper, but these sorts of inquiries can help us dig up the spirit of pragmatism in our lives and churches.

This may seem to some like making much ado about nothing, but remember: The leaven of pragmatism in our spiritual and religious thinking is a spirit of worldliness. As such, pragmatism is in opposition to the spirit of the gospel.

Interestingly enough, however, while pragmatic thinking in our lives and churches so often manifests itself in a spirit of licentiousness, it is actually not fundamentally different from religious legalism! Both pragmatism and legalism function in formulaic ways; both see human exertion or know-how as the mechanism for justification. Both are basically self-salvation projects.

Worldliness and legalism may be two different categories of expression, but both are operations of the flesh. Thus, neither is the antidote to the other. Only centering on the gospel will keep us from drifting into the ditches on either side. And it is on the other ditch that we will now focus our caution.

Chapter Seven

# Less than Free

## *A Drift into the New Legalism*

*And he cautioned them, saying, "Watch out;*
*beware of the leaven of the Pharisees."*
**—Mark 8:15**

**THE LEAVEN OF LEGALISM IS SUBTLER THAN WE REALIZE.**
For years I ministerially operated as a legalist all the while
believing I had escaped it. If you had given me a theological
exam to test my background doctrine, I would have scored as
orthodox in my view of justification by grace alone through
faith alone in Christ alone. But functionally and method-
ologically, my doctrine was not directing my ministry. This
disorder is intrinsic to the attractional paradigm.

The genesis of "seeker church" ministry was predicated
on a rejection of what was viewed as rigid fundamentalism,
dry doctrine, and culturally irrelevant application. Early
practitioners of the seeker church saw themselves as moving
beyond the legalism of the traditional church and pioneering a more gracious approach to evangelism proper and the
Christian life in general. Imagine the shock, then, of so many
of us who gradually came to the realization we had not really
left behind the spirit of legalism at all.

In my preaching and in my worship, I intended grace in
my shift from the "thou shalt nots" to more positive application. Instead of constantly preaching what folks needed
to stay away from in order to avoid condemnation, I began
preaching what they needed to do in order to become more
spiritually healthy and successful people. My sermons, once
populated with theoretical doctrine, became preoccupied
with "action steps." The intent was to show how the Bible is
relevant to everyday life; the effect was to create a new set of
priorities for Christians and non-Christians alike that aligned
more with "God's wonderful plan for your life."

My churches loosened up the dress code. We modernized the aesthetic. We hipped up the music. But we kept the moralism. We just made it more aspirational, more therapeutic, and less "religious."

For me, this realization came in waves as I grew more and more disillusioned with the endless pointers, steps, and practicalities. Our law might have been more positive than our grandfathers', but it wasn't any less *law*. I also became aware of how little impact all the practical application seemed to have on the people we were trying to reach. As the gospel itself began to recede into the background, I witnessed how all the practical stuff wasn't resulting in a holier church. I also realized that we weren't effectively reaching the people we claimed to care most about: the unchurched. The data from the emerging research into the seeker church movement began to bear that out.[1]

I also began to see the ineffectiveness of focusing on practical application in my own life. In the early 2000s I experienced a personal train wreck. My marriage was broken and on the verge of divorce. I was plunged into a long period of deep depression. I battled suicidal thoughts constantly. At the time, I was neck-deep in the attractional church and had fully bought in to its aims and methods. Not only had I prioritized positive law in my ministry up to that point, but I had a notebook full of sermon notes from others giving me hundreds of action steps to be a better, more highly functioning person

---

1. See in particular the coverage of Sally Morgenthaler's work, as well as the results of Willow Creek's REVEAL survey, among other research notes in Jared C. Wilson, *The Prodigal Church: A Gentle Manifesto against the Status Quo* (Wheaton, IL: Crossway, 2015).

according to biblical principles. Yet none of those steps could fulfill the inconsolable ache inside of me. All the casual dress, cool music, and focus on practical application did not keep me from being a legalist at heart, and thus they could not keep me from despairing of life itself.

In the midst of that terrible season, I was awakened to the centrality of the gospel. It did not come about through any particular sermon. It did not come about by being given a particular book or being taken to a particular conference. I wasn't aware of any evangelical movement outside my own. But the Lord was kind enough to arrest my attention through my affliction and redirect me to the old, old story of the cross of Christ. I discovered that the news I thought was just for lost people was the power of salvation for *the found* as well.

It was out of that "gospel wakefulness" experience that the Lord kindly restored my marriage and renewed my spirit and began to reform my thinking about church and ministry. For one thing, it dawned on me for the first time that trying to attract (and keep) unbelievers with law (even if it was positive) was exactly backward from the Bible's perspective. The attractional church has failed to keep law and gospel distinguished, and it has failed to keep them in the right order. To heap imperatives upon unbelievers can, at best, only create self-righteous unbelievers. People change by grace, not law.

A commitment to the principle of gospel-centrality is a ruiner of attractional ministry. It takes our orthodox allegiance to salvation by grace alone and mobilizes it in our preaching and teaching. It also ought to shape our relationships and fellowships, because it is quite possible to put the letter of grace in our formal faith statements while still operating in a spirit of law.

And the attractional church is not the only place we see this disorder at work. Evangelicalism as a whole, even the confessionally Reformed parts, is constantly lured away from gospel-centrality into legalism.

The new, subtler legalism is informal and operates more as a relational and social disorder than as a matter of doctrine.

When Jesus says to his disciples, "Watch out; beware of the leaven of the Pharisees" (Mark 8:15), he is not warning them about "religion." That is a facile take, quite common among evangelicals who have come to see the Pharisees as merely representing "religious people." No, he is warning them about Christless religion, about the erecting of codes and cultures that prioritize outward conformity (even to something good like God's law!) over against the preeminence of themselves. The Pharisees' primary problem, after all, was not that they were religious, but that they had rejected the center of true religion, which is Christ himself.

We see the new legalism at work in evangelicalism today when we conflate secondary and even tertiary doctrines with primary ones. We see it at work when we prioritize cultural conformity over gospel unity and insist on extrabiblical litmus tests for orthodoxy that are more in line with tribal affiliations than with Christian communion.

It is no wonder, then, that as the new legalism spreads among us, we begin operating in a mode of suspicion, with an out-of-biblical-proportion concern about who's in and who's out.

# The Fundamentalist Impulse

The fundamentalists were not formal legalists. Indeed, the early fundamentalist movement was originally about recommitting to the truths of Scripture and resisting the compromising influence of modernism. But as the historic fundamentalists were more and more galvanized around what they were against, it became harder and harder to discern what they were actually for. Fundamentalism became less about its doctrine and more about its culture. The spirit of fundamentalism today is the fruit of an isolating and insular focus on law over grace.

Carl F. H. Henry wrote the book on evangelical fundamentalism. In his now-classic *The Uneasy Conscience of Modern Fundamentalism*, he noted the assumptions and tendencies of the movement that gave rise to fundamentalist culture. He writes, for instance, "The problem of Fundamentalism then is basically not one of finding a valid message, but rather of giving the redemptive world a proper temporal focus."[2] Henry insists that fundamentalism's lack of interest in social justice, kingdom perspective, and eschatological presentism contributes to an unhealthy inwardness and cynicism. He writes later, "The redemptive message has implications for all of life; a truncated life results from a truncated message."[3]

The emphasis of gospel-centrality is that the redemptive message of the gospel is to be the center of all of life. The fundamentalist spirit is more about ticking the right cultural boxes than about the gospel. Centering on non-gospel

---

2. Carl F. H. Henry, *The Uneasy Conscience of Modern Fundamentalism* (1947; Grand Rapids: Eerdmans, 2003), 62.

3. Henry, *Uneasy Conscience*, 65.

ideologies cultivates a relational legalism that leads to inevitable dissolutions. (I think of how the social justice conversation became the issue of division for many evangelicals who once felt "together for the gospel.") The fundamentalist spirit quenches the spirit of the gospel. The result is a disordered culture—a kind of *antisocial* culture.

Thus, the fundamentalist spirit today transcends formal religious environments. It is not only religious people who are vulnerable to pharisaical leaven. We've certainly seen the fundamentalist spirit in the radical conservatism of those we'd consider right wing, but we're also seeing it more and more in the illiberal liberalism among the left wing. Cancel culture crosses the religious and political spectra, as do uneasy alliances formed by shared antagonism.

Centering on non-gospel ideologies will also align you with some surprising allies. When North Point Community Church's Andy Stanley hosted a conference on LGBTQ+ issues at his church and invited only gay-affirming speakers, many evangelicals were shocked, while others saw the development as simply downstream from his increasing rejection of biblicism. The one thing that seemed to unite Stanley with this array of heterodox speakers—apart from his apparent compromise on the biblical sexual ethic—was their antagonism toward conservative evangelical leaders.[4]

On the other end of the spectrum, many have noticed the increasing divisions among the "social justice contras," who once aligned firmly in their stances against critical

---

4. Ian M. Giatti, "Andy Stanley Defends Conference for Parents of 'Gay Kids,' Says Homosexuality Is Not a 'Behavior,' but a 'Defining Attraction,'" *Christian Post*, October 3, 2023, https://www.christianpost.com/news/andy-stanley-defends-conference-for-parents-of-gay-kids.html.

race theory and radical feminism and the like, yet are now descending into constant intramural squabbles over Christian nationalism and antisemitism.

Alignments formed in the fundamentalist spirit always backfire, as the impulse is to police for cultural correctness, always drawing the circles smaller and smaller around the truly faithful.

The fundamentalist impulse is legalistic at heart—even if not in doctrine—because it is always testing and policing according to informal cultural standards. It operates in a spirit of suspicion. It cultivates a climate of law, not of grace. Even in the pursuit of good and biblical things, we can inadvertently give purchase to the leaven of legalism when we prioritize external standards over the power of grace. All of this is the result of ordering the gospel's implications over the gospel itself. D. A. Carson writes,

> The gospel has both purposes and entailments in human conduct. The entailments must be preached. But if you preach the entailments as if they were the gospel itself, pretty soon you lose sight of the reality of the gospel—that it is the good news of what God has done, not a description of what we ought to do in consequence. Pretty soon the gospel descends to mere moralism. One cannot too forcefully insist on the distinction between the gospel and its entailments.[5]

At the risk of belaboring the point, this distinction is important not just to ensure orthodoxy on paper, but to ensure

---

5. D. A. Carson, *The Gospel and the Modern World: A Theological Vision for the Church*, ed. Brian J. Tabb (Wheaton, IL: Crossway, 2023), 94.

our orthodoxy is truly central and thus produces the right entailments!

## Legalism on Paper versus Legalism in Person

The new legalism is informal and operates more as a relational and social disorder than as a matter of doctrine. It is often denied "on paper" but then evidenced in ministry emphases and personal passions. We can un-say with our demeanor what we say with our doctrine.

Commenting on Sinclair Ferguson's analysis of the Church of Scotland's Marrow Controversy of the 1700s, Tim Keller writes,

> The first and inarguable conclusion is that *legalism and antinomianism are much more than doctrinal positions.* Neither side in the Marrow Controversy was saying, "You can save yourself through works," or, "Once you are saved, you don't have to obey the law of God." Neither side subscribed to overt, explicit legalistic or antinomian doctrine. Nonetheless, legalism and antinomianism can be strongly present in a ministry. Each is a web of attitudes of heart, practices, character, and ways of reading Scripture. At one point Sinclair even says, rightly, that a legal spirit consists in part in how you *feel* toward God.[6]

---

6. Timothy Keller, foreword to *The Whole Christ: Legalism, Antinomianism, and Gospel Assurance; Why the Marrow Controversy Still Matters*, by Sinclair B. Ferguson (Wheaton, IL: Crossway, 2016), 12–13, emphasis original.

I have heard it said and believe it to be true that people don't simply become passionate about what a teacher tells them to be passionate about; they become passionate about what a teacher is evidently passionate about. Thus, if we are gospel-centered on paper but legalistic in person, those we teach and shepherd will be much more impacted by legalism than gospel-centrality. If our emphases and energies trend more toward the law than grace, we will inadvertently form our churches and our other relationships in the way of legalism.

Ferguson offers his own sort of diagnostic analyses for the preacher's self-reflection:

> Is it obvious to me, and of engrossing concern, that the chief focus, the dominant note in the sermons I preach (or hear), is "Jesus Christ and him crucified"? Or is the dominant emphasis (and perhaps the greatest energies of the preacher?) focused somewhere else, perhaps on how to overcome sin, or how to live the Christian life, or on the benefits to be received from the gospel? All are legitimate emphases in their place, but that place is never center stage.[7]

The spirit of the law certainly dominates the teaching of the attractional church, which as a matter of intention prioritizes practical application over the preaching of Christ crucified. But it may also dominate the teaching of some of our favorite "doctrinal preachers," the ones who labor intensively in exegesis and exposition and then present sermons that are preoccupied with substantive theological truths

---

7. Ferguson, *Whole Christ*, 50.

and passionate exhortations to holiness for which the finished work of Christ functions latently or as a homiletical afterthought.

Some of the Reformed world's favorite celebrity preachers have been those who would never in a million years affirm works righteousness but marshal their most passionate and earnest rhetoric around the works of the law. They may not be legalists on paper, but they appear so in the pulpit.

To put it another way, why—if the unique treasure of Christianity is the good news—does so much of our preaching and teaching seem to indicate that the bad news is more important?

Ray Ortlund Jr. warns us, "It is possible to hold to the gospel as a theory even as we lose it as a reality."[8]

We must be very careful—watch out!—for the leaven of the Pharisees in our life and ministry. This is as much a part of keeping a close watch on our life and doctrine as is all the rest of biblical orthodoxy. This is what makes the drift into the new legalism so dangerous. We may not be legalists on paper, but we can adopt the spirit of legalism in person.

## Putting the Law in Its Place

Certainly the good news will only be as good as the bad news is bad. The answer to a legalistic spirit is not an antinomian spirit! Remember, the call is not to pursue a kind of "balance" in this way. Rather, it is to remember, in the sense

---

8. Ray Ortlund, *The Gospel: How the Church Portrays the Beauty of Christ*, Building Healthy Churches (Wheaton, IL: Crossway, 2014), 88.

of 2 Corinthians 3, that the gospel is indeed the "ministry of righteousness" and that in fact its glory *surpasses* the glory of the "ministry of condemnation" (v. 9).

In Romans 3:19–26, the apostle Paul writes,

> Now we know that whatever the law says it speaks to those who are under the law, so that every mouth may be stopped, and the whole world may be held accountable to God. For by works of the law no human being will be justified in his sight, since through the law comes knowledge of sin.
>
> But now the righteousness of God has been manifested apart from the law, although the Law and the Prophets bear witness to it—the righteousness of God through faith in Jesus Christ for all who believe. For there is no distinction: for all have sinned and fall short of the glory of God, and are justified by his grace as a gift, through the redemption that is in Christ Jesus, whom God put forward as a propitiation by his blood, to be received by faith. This was to show God's righteousness, because in his divine forbearance he had passed over former sins. It was to show his righteousness at the present time, so that he might be just and the justifier of the one who has faith in Jesus.

The gospel as good news should not exist for us merely as an idea or a theory or an academic philosophy. As Ortlund says, "The gospel does not hang in midair as an abstraction."[9]

So we must take grace *personally*, if we're going to take it at all. This has perhaps been the greatest failure of the

9. Ortlund, *Gospel*, 65.

gospel-centered movement: that gospel-centrality would simply constitute the latest evangelical fad or theological preoccupation. Now, to be honest, there are a lot worse things to be preoccupied with! But the gospel cannot save a single soul as an abstraction. Nor should those of us who claim it imagine for one second we are justified by appreciation alone.

Christ Jesus the Lord only deals with us on the playing field of reality. And so our gospel must be primarily on that field, or it will do us no good.

This is what Paul is doing in Romans 3, when he takes the high-minded talk on God's glory and man's sin and lays these realities upon the reader's soul. We see in that passage that the law's function is good in design.

Remember that gospel-centrism is not gospel-onlyism! To be gospel-centered is not to be law-neglecting. Nor is it to be law-*flippant*.

How can we be flippant about what Paul has taken great pains to declare as righteous, spilling much ink by the inspiration of the Spirit? To be flippant about the law is to be flippant about the Word of the Spirit.

Make no mistake: The law cannot do what the gospel does. But the law is not bad. It is good. It is good at what it is designed to do.

Paul says in verse 19 that "every mouth may be stopped" in being held accountable to God. This wording is perhaps an allusion to Job 40:4, when, in his unique answer to Job's questions, God takes the sufferer through a whirlwind tour of nature, showing his glory, and Job responds, "Behold, I am of small account; what shall I answer you? I lay my hand on my mouth."

Several years ago, as I was doing some preaching in Australia, one of our hosts took my wife and me for an afternoon at the beach. Becky and I were enjoying a casual stroll around some rocky cliffs, pausing to dip our hands in little tide pools and exploring all the stony crags and crevasses that led out over a roiling ocean. We wandered carelessly to the edge of the rocky ledge, against which foamy waves were crashing. The sea spray wet our faces. In an instant, however, a rogue wave came roaring over the edge and swallowed up the ledge between us and the safety of the beach. I was knocked over and fell into a hole in the rocks that I could not see because the shallows had engulfed it.

All I pictured in that moment was the water rapidly receding and sweeping us off the cliff and into the dangerous sea.

I clambered desperately out of the crevasse and ran haphazardly to the other side before the current could seize us. My legs were covered in bloody lacerations, as I could not carefully navigate the cracks and ridges in my haste to get back to safety.

I should note at this point that my wife was laughing the entire time. She did not sense any danger in this scenario at all! In fact, she had remained calm and slowly navigated her way to the sand.

But when we finally reunited with our host, and I explained the situation to him, his face went white. "Do you know how many tourists get swept out into the ocean and drown exactly because of things like this?" He was afraid he'd be responsible for losing his American guests! He apologized for not warning us and chauffeured us back to the venue.

In that moment, I experienced a natural corollary to the

mouth-stopping power of the law. I was casually and haphazardly disrespecting the forces around me, sauntering around without a care in the world, and then—bam!—the crashing wave shut me up.

The word of the law is like that. We are minding our business, kings of the world, lords of our own lives, and then we are confronted by the reality of God, and it stops us, silences us, and wrecks our sense of self-sufficiency. It quiets us, stifles us. It makes us accountable.

The way it does this is twofold. It reveals the holiness of God and, by doing so, reveals our utter unholiness. The law makes a mockery of both the licentious and the legalist.

No, we ought never be flippant about God's law. God himself certainly isn't.

The only right disposition in response to a vision of God's holiness is to see our own fallenness and then to *feel* fallen. Because the law's indictment of us is total in impact.

The import of the law is utterly decimating. Paul is clear in Romans 3:20: "For by works of the law no human being will be justified in his sight, since through the law comes knowledge of sin."

Once, at another speaking engagement, a fellow approached me after my message to ask a question about obedience. He said, "I've searched myself inside and out. I've become aware of every sin in my life, and I've repented of them all."

"You're totally repentant?" I asked.

"Yes," he replied. "What is there left for me to do?"

I told him to repent of his repentance.

He'd made a mockery of the law by thinking he had it

beat. This is the ironic condemnation embedded in any kind of legalism. As soon as you find the law manageable or accomplishable, you reveal your own pride and self-righteousness.

This is why Luther's first thesis is that the believer's whole life is to be one of repentance. It posits repentance as an ongoing process, a daily commitment. The law doesn't just condemn us; it condemns us thoroughly. Nothing is outside the fallout zone of the law's atomic destruction. It affects all people—"all have sinned" (Rom. 3:23)—and it affects all people *all the way through*.

This is what frustrates our conception of obedience even after our conversion. None of our motives are unmixed. None of our motivations are undiluted. Nobody's faith is perfect.

The good news is only as good as the bad news is bad. And while those captured by the spirit of legalism may insist upon highlighting holiness and commanding good works, without the preeminence of the gospel, they're actually insinuating the law is "doable." It then ceases to be bad news. It's not bad news if you can kinda sorta make it.

But if you are utterly bad, the good news is full of grace.

In the gospel, even our imperfect faith becomes credited to us as perfect righteousness. Because it is not a perfect faith that saves but a *true* faith. It's not a strong faith that saves but a strong Savior.

## Accomplishing the Law

Paul writes, "But now the righteousness of God has been manifested apart from the law, although the Law and the Prophets bear witness to it—the righteousness of God through faith in Jesus Christ for all who believe" (Rom. 3:21–22).

The spirit of legalism will be defeated if we more loudly and passionately declare that the law has been fulfilled in Christ. The righteousness of God has been manifested!

I don't know if you see the conundrum that may arise from this, but it reveals something deeper and more beautiful about the gospel than the simple "forgiveness of sins" that is at the crux of the matter. Paul is not saying Christ's sacrifice falls short of manifesting the righteousness of God. He's not saying salvation is accomplished with no respect at all to the law.

Attractional church celebrity Steven Furtick went viral a few years ago for a sermon clip in which he claimed that God broke the law out of love for us.[10] But I believe this claim is theologically confused; while it aims to make much of the gospel, it is actually gospel ignorant. Our righteousness is manifested apart from the law because none of us can be justified by our works. But Christ's righteousness was manifested in keeping the law, both in his sinless life and in his sacrificial death. Keeping the law was precisely what Christ was doing on the cross.

In this sense we *are* saved by works—just not our own!

Consequently, we can see another level of depth in the good news in Romans 3:24: We are justified by his grace as a gift. We aren't just gifted forgiveness, as wonderful as that

---

10. Steven Furtick, "God Broke the Law for Love," Facebook video, March 29, 2016, https://www.facebook.com/watch/?v=1093531844001563. See my full thoughts on this sermon clip at Jared C. Wilson, "God Broke Antinomianism for Love," The Gospel Coalition, April 6, 2016, https://www.thegospelcoalition .org/article/god-broke-antinonianism-for-love/.

is. We are gifted forgiveness *and* the perfect righteousness of Christ.

Justification and imputation are a package deal.

Abraham believed God, and it was credited to him not as a blank slate, but as righteousness (Rom. 4:3).

In fact, the imputation of Christ's righteousness becomes the new reality for the Christian. It fundamentally changes who we are at our insidest insides. "If anyone is in Christ, he is a new creation. The old has passed away; behold, the new has come" (2 Cor. 5:17).

So his righteousness becomes our righteousness. He no longer remembers our sin.

In this way, Saint Augustine could boldly say, "Grace is given in order that Law might be fulfilled."[11]

This, by the way, is what makes sin so egregious for the Christian—more so than for the non-Christian. For the Christian, to sin is to go against his or her new nature. And this is true especially for the sin of legalism. It is not just a spirit of disobedience toward God; it is a blasphemy against his gospel and a perversion of his law.

By faith, the law's curse is vanquished. The law is accomplished for us by Christ.

God doesn't bend his rules. That's antinomianism. And God's rules aren't manageable. That's legalism. Instead, "God put forward [Christ Jesus] as a propitiation by his blood, to be received by faith. This was to show God's righteousness, because in his divine forbearance he had passed over former sins" (Rom. 3:25).

---

11. Augustine, *On the Spirit and the Letter*, trans. W. J. Sparrow Simpson (London: Macmillan, 1925), 23.

If we are justified by our faith, we have received the righteousness of Christ so that at the present time—and for all time—we may be counted righteous in Christ. The curse of the law has been taken from us, put on Christ, buried with him in his death, buried still while he is resurrected, and canceled for all time.

This news is the most staggering and startling reality of all time. To regularly eclipse its glory in our ministries with the lesser glory of the law's commandments is to distort the gospel and deform God's people.

Let us "[fix] our eyes on Jesus, the pioneer and perfecter of faith" (Heb. 12:2 NIV). If we do, we can run straight the race before us. If we do not, we will drift to one side or the other.

Chapter Eight

# Paying Closer Attention

*Alerted Not to Drift*

*Only let us hold true*
*to what we have attained.*
**—Philippians 3:16**

HAS IT EVER OCCURRED TO YOU HOW, FOR EVERY CHURCH context and circumstance Paul addresses in his epistles, his remedy for each is essentially the same?

The issues:

- The Roman church is suffering from threats to unity—theologically, socially, and missionally.
- The Corinthians are corrupted by sensuality and other compromise and roiled by divisions.
- The Galatians are falling prey to the Judaizer heresy of works righteousness.
- The Ephesians are experiencing a garden variety of issues among multiple churches.
- The Philippians are troubled by disunity but also by the presence of suffering.
- The Colossians may be influenced by false teaching that denies the deity of Christ.
- The Thessalonians are undergoing persecution.

His responses:

- "So I am eager to preach the gospel to you also who are in Rome" (Rom. 1:15).
- "Now I would remind you, brothers, of the gospel I preached to you, which you received, in which you stand, and by which you are being saved, if you hold fast to the word I preached to you—unless you believed

in vain. For I delivered to you as of first importance what I also received" (1 Cor. 15:1–3).

- "For all the promises of God find their Yes in him. That is why it is through him that we utter our Amen to God for his glory. And it is God who establishes us with you in Christ, and has anointed us, and who has also put his seal on us and given us his Spirit in our hearts as a guarantee" (2 Cor. 1:20–22).

- "I am astonished that you are so quickly deserting him who called you in the grace of Christ and are turning to a different gospel. . . . To them we did not yield in submission even for a moment, so that the truth of the gospel might be preserved for you" (Gal. 1:6; 2:5).

- "For this reason, because I have heard of your faith in the Lord Jesus and your love toward all the saints, I do not cease to give thanks for you, remembering you in my prayers, that the God of our Lord Jesus Christ, the Father of glory, may give you the Spirit of wisdom and of revelation in the knowledge of him, having the eyes of your hearts enlightened, that you may know what is the hope to which he has called you, what are the riches of his glorious inheritance in the saints, and what is the immeasurable greatness of his power toward us who believe, according to the working of his great might that he worked in Christ when he raised him from the dead and seated him at his right hand in the heavenly places" (Eph. 1:15–20).

- "Only let your manner of life be worthy of the gospel of Christ, so that whether I come and see you or am absent, I may hear of you that you are standing firm in one spirit, with one mind striving side by side for the faith of the gospel" (Phil. 1:27).

- "... continue in the faith, stable and steadfast, not shifting from the hope of the gospel that you heard" (Col. 1:23).
- "But though we had already suffered and been shamefully treated at Philippi, as you know, we had boldness in our God to declare to you the gospel of God in the midst of much conflict" (1 Thess. 2:2).
- "To this he called you through our gospel, so that you may obtain the glory of our Lord Jesus Christ" (2 Thess. 2:14).

At every point, to every church, his directive is basically the same: Your first attention must be to the gospel. Every church also receives practical exhortations—instructions applied to each directly (and to all Christians by implication)—but even those flow from the indicatives of the finished work of Christ. He frequently highlights a different facet of the gospel message in his letters to each church, but he never offers one philosophy to one church and a different philosophy to another.

Paul does not seem to traffic at all in ministry strategies. His central commandment is always to return to the central proclamation: "For I decided to know nothing among you except Jesus Christ and him crucified" (1 Cor. 2:2). "Only let us hold true to what we have attained" (Phil. 3:16).

The primary reason we ought to commit to gospel-centeredness rather than law-centeredness is because God commands it! Our first obedience should be to the gospel (2 Thess. 1:8; 1 Peter 4:17).

Now that we have faced our propensity for drift and examined various departure dangers, how can we stand firm and make sure we are not susceptible to them? Here I will review the substance and implications of the concept of gospel-centrality and explain why the evangelical commitment to *semper reformanda* requires our fidelity to gospel-centrality.

If we want to see spiritual renewal, and even revival, in our day we will need to embrace a spirit of repentance and a radical recommitment to the One whose grace has redeemed us.

## Robustly Gospel-Centered Gatherings

"Let the word of Christ dwell in you richly," Paul writes in Colossians 3:16, "teaching and admonishing one another in all wisdom, singing psalms and hymns and spiritual songs, with thankfulness in your hearts to God."

The scope of this verse isn't limited to the consideration of a worship service, but it certainly includes that consideration. Notice the source of the teaching, admonishing, singing, and thanksgiving—all typical elements of a Christian church service. It is *the word of Christ dwelling in us richly.*

The evangelical church in the west is in desperate need of a reclamation of this richly dwelling Word. Many of us use the Word, but not to the point of richness or indwelling. If the church is the new humanity made by God through his gospel—and not simply a religious resource center where we wet our spiritual whistles—we have no other business than to gather around the glory of the grace of God and *stare at it* until we are changed.

This is not possible when our churches reserve the gospel for special occasions, use it as a flavor in the service, or otherwise relegate it to a formality or formulaic recitation. The good news of Jesus is central enough, resilient enough, and powerful enough to be the main thing in our worship.

Our preaching, singing, liturgy, and ordinances, then, are to be intentionally and explicitly gospel-centered.

If the whole Bible is about Jesus, if people change by grace and not by law, and if our ultimate validation comes from Christ's performance rather than our own, then our sermons ought to be relentlessly devoted to preaching Christ as preeminent over all things, brimming with grace, and loaded with the comfort that comes from the announcement of justification by faith.

If these principles of gospel-centrality are biblical, then our songs ought to help us rehearse over and over again the marvelous grace of our loving Lord, extol the wonders of his love, and shift the knowledge of the riches of his loving-kindness from our heads into our hearts.

If gospel-centrality is worth committing to, it's worth conforming our liturgy to it. We should examine our entire worship service to make sure the elements, the order, the whole "vibe," if you will, leaves the overwhelming impression that the most important takeaway is that Christ took away our sin and cast it as far as the east is from the west.

If our first imperative is to return to the indicative, we should feel burdened for more credible baptisms in our church—that is, baptism less "for show," less about sentimental religious expression or accumulating spurious numbers, and more about authentic professions of faith from evangelized persons. We should pray our guts out and evangelize our feet off in order that the gospel would manifest more visibly through professions of faith. We should examine the way in which we receive the Lord's Supper—or, for some of us, the *frequency* with which we receive it—to make sure we have not relegated this direct proclamation of the good news (1 Cor. 11:26) to either perfunctory or neglected observance.

The Lord's Supper is a tangible grace of the gospel given to us by Jesus himself. It is a real means of grace to his church—not in a mediatory or meritorious way, but in a spiritually strengthening way. Just as the faithful preaching of God's Word edifies our souls with grace, the eating of the bread and drinking of the cup also edifies our souls with grace, because the Supper *is* a faithful preaching of God's Word.

The aim in all of these efforts is to ensure that the gospel directly and robustly informs our worship. Paul's language in 1 Corinthians 15:1–2 tells us that the gospel is the grounds of our past conversion, our present standing before God, and our ongoing sanctification by his Spirit, all the way to our future glorification.

Orienting our worship around a million other things may make us feel more courageous, intelligent, prophetic, comfortable, or inspired, but these feelings could be an indicator that we are drifting away from the gospel. We may not even notice it, because we're using the Bible and singing songs to God. We may not notice it, because the building is full and people are enthusiastic. We may not notice it, because our platform is growing and we get lots of pats on the back from our fellow tribesmen. We may not notice it, because the leaders of our opposition tribes are themselves off-target, and we are proud of not being like them. We may not notice it, because we've hitched ourselves to something good, even something adjacent to the gospel.

But without a strong connection to the anchor of grace, we will be carried away, however slowly and imperceptibly, by the currents around us.

Can the gospel bear the weight of eternal life? Is it sturdy enough to save and preserve a sinner for all eternity? Yes! And if the gospel is big enough to be the grounds of our salvation for all eternity, surely it will be enough for a lifetime of Sundays. Indeed, like manna in the desert, the gospel's heavenly bread will be more than enough for every day.

What we are aiming for in our worship gatherings—and all the other myriad gatherings of the local church from Sunday school to small groups to all the little informal fellowships scattered throughout—is a conscious reevangelization of the people of God. No Christian loses their salvation, of course, but we can certainly lose our mindfulness of it. And our heart for it. So the purpose of the church's gatherings is to recenter us and reorganize us over and over again around the finished work of Christ.

Dietrich Bonhoeffer said, "We meet one another as bringers of the message of salvation."[1]

There should really be no other explanation for church.

In the words of the original Lutheran,

---

1. Dietrich Bonhoeffer, *Life Together* (New York: Harper & Row, 1954), 23.

Here I must take counsel of the gospel. I must hearken to the gospel, which teacheth me, not what I ought to do, (for that is the proper office of the law), but what Jesus Christ the Son of God hath done for me: to wit, that He suffered and died to deliver me from sin and death. The gospel willeth me to receive this, and to believe it. And this is the truth of the gospel. It is also the principal article of all Christian doctrine, wherein the knowledge of all godliness consisteth. Most necessary it is, therefore, that we should know this article well, teach it unto others, and beat it into their heads continually.[2]

Now, this is counterintuitive for many, especially those concerned about Christian holiness in a world of temptation and Christian courage in a world of hostility toward faith and oppressive immorality. But remember, the Scriptures never position the law as empowering anything but our sense of condemnation. "It is good for the heart to be strengthened by grace" (Heb. 13:9).

The word of grace that saved us can be trusted to preserve us. John Owen reflects,

A man would think it were a more difficult work to convert men from Judaism, or paganism, or any false religion, unto the profession of the gospel, than to retain them in that profession when they are initiated thereinto. For in that first work there are all sorts of prejudices and difficulties to be conflicted withal; and not the least advantage

---

2. Martin Luther, *St. Paul's Epistle to the Galatians* (Philadelphia: Smith, English, 1860), 206.

from any acknowledged principles of truth. But as to the preservation of men in the profession of the truth which they have received and owned, the work on many accounts seems to be more expedite and easy. If therefore the dispensation of the word as it is God's ordinance unto that end, has been a sufficient and effectual means for the former, what reason can be assigned that it should not be so for the latter also, without farther force or violence?[3]

Is it the ongoing work of Christian discipleship unto spiritual holiness you're concerned about? "Rest assured," Spurgeon echoes, "if motives fetched from the gospel will not kill sin, motives fetched from the law never will."[4]

The most courageous, prophetic, and countercultural thing ministry leaders can do is stubbornly and joyfully center their churches around the gospel.

## Gospel-Centered in Person, Not Just in Paradigm

Whatever her pastors are, a church will become. If we do not much find the gospel resilient, over time our people won't either. If we do not find it a versatile resource, neither will our congregation.

Similarly, if we talk the talk but do not walk the walk, our church will become accustomed to doing the same.

---

3. John Owen, *Apostasy from the Gospel*, in *The Complete Works of John Owen*, vol. 14 (Wheaton, IL: Crossway, 2023), 196–97.

4. Charles Spurgeon, "The Fourfold Treasure," in *The Metropolitan Tabernacle Pulpit*, vol. 17 (London: Passmore & Alabaster, 1872), 286.

Whole churches can learn to speak gospel-ese while knowing little about the claims of gospel-centrality or their theological import. "Gospel-centeredness" just becomes the community's lingo. Worse still, when that happens, a church can operate functionally in a judgmental climate of law—overrun by gossip and suspicion, populated with people jockeying for position or lamenting their lack thereof—while gospel stuff dominates the marketing, media, and messaging of the church.

It is especially damaging, I think, when leaders known publicly for demonstrating grace are exposed as graceless behind the scenes. It doesn't just bring the leader into disrepute; it tarnishes the public perception of the gospel itself. When the brash public firebrand makes a mess of his life and ministry, I am saddened but not usually surprised. But when a fellow widely known for his sweetness and gentleness is revealed to be a bully, charlatan, or sexual deviant, my heart truly drops.

As I write this, another "gospel-centered" pastor has been exposed for his disqualifying double life. A pastor known for his gracious demeanor and joyful personality is revealed to be a predator.

Maybe your situation is not so dire. You are not engaged in sexual sin, financial greed, aggressive short-temperedness, or some other obviously disqualifying sin, but you're just . . . going through the motions. You're talking the talk, but behind the scenes you are spiritually dry. You are shepherding "out of compulsion" (1 Peter 5:2 CSB). You've essentially become a hired hand (John 10:12–13). You're gospel-centered in paradigm (in public) but not in private (in person).

If I speak the language of gospel-centrality but do not have love, the paradigm will sound like nothing more than a clanging cymbal (1 Cor. 13:1).

It is important that we do not conduct a relationship with Jesus *as an idea* rather than as an actual person. Since the fad has run its course, a commitment to gospel-centrality only on paper doesn't make sense in these days of evangelical distaste for it. If you're going to commit to it, commit to it *through Jesus*.

If I could offer one more sign of potential drift in this regard, it would be abundant "gospel talk" without much articulation of the actual gospel. I see this in a lot of preachers who use the word *gospel* a lot while rarely explaining the gospel's word. Their sermons and writings are peppered with phrases like "believe in the gospel," "center on the gospel," and "lean into the gospel." They also use *gospel* as an adjective or modifier quite a bit: "gospel-centered," "gospel-driven," "gospel issues," "gospel community," "gospel mission."

This phenomenon is rather deceptive. It gives the appearance of substantive gospel content but actually empties the gospel of its power to transform. Remember that the word *gospel* isn't magic. The word *gospel* doesn't *do* anything. We have to actually articulate the good news—the cross and resurrection of Jesus at bare minimum—in order to experience real power.

Preacher, you may wonder why, despite all your gospely sermons, your people are not growing in holiness or missional zeal. But I challenge you to withstand the temptation to think gospel-centrality doesn't work. The Holy Spirit working through the message of the good news operates on his own timetable, not ours. Have exceeding patience with your people, and perhaps use it as a motivator to reevaluate your assumptions about your preaching. Is it possible you're giving people lots of good news jargon without the actual good news?

I realized once that I had fallen into a pattern of being "legalistic" about gospel-centrality! My preaching, particularly my conclusions, became routinely riddled with admonitions to my people to "be gospel-centered" and "center on the gospel." These are indeed important imperatives, but divorced from the indicative of the gospel itself, they cannot actually be heeded. Since that realization, I remind myself not simply to *tell* people about the glory of Christ but to do my best to *show* it to them. It's one thing to say, "Jesus is glorious; be in awe of him." It's another to preach Jesus in such a way that your hearers are confronted with a vision of his glory and put in a position of awe.

Who the pastor is outside the pulpit is equally important, of course. In the areas of leadership and shepherding, if we are not rehearsing the message of Christ's cross and resurrection with our fellow pastors, staff, friends, family, and the rest of our flock, we are in real danger of drifting away from our first love. In another counterintuitive truth, the pastor who is constantly digging in his ministerial tool kit to dispense practical wisdom and personal insights will find himself often scraping up the reserves of his own heart and energy. Our internal resources are finite. But if we make it a point to direct people away from ourselves and to Jesus, we will find that his fullness is an endless fountain of grace (John 1:16).

The gospel-centered pastor in the counseling room, living room, and board room will discover again and again

Christ's miracle of provision. David Hansen says, "The gospel is the power of the love of God to give to others. If the gospel is the pastor's bread, the pastor will always have bread to give away."[5]

This is the right order for our interpersonal fellowship as well. Nothing is as powerful as a community of sinners brought together—because of Jesus—and actually *enjoying* having been brought together because of Jesus.

It is nice to have multiple things in common with our brothers and sisters in Christ. But in the church, the only thing we *must* have in common is an interest in the grace that redeemed us. As such, a truly gospel-centered Christian will not focus on all the ways he is different from others in the church, or all the ways others in the church are different from him.

When we are gospel-centered in person, we consider our preferences to be incidental and our biases to be hindrances to authentic gospel-centered community. With the Holy Spirit's help, when we actually center on the gospel, we see the wisdom and wonder of a portrait of community like we see in Romans 15:1–7:

> We who are strong have an obligation to bear with the failings of the weak, and not to please ourselves. Let each of us please his neighbor for his good, to build him up. For Christ did not please himself, but as it is written, "The reproaches of those who reproached you fell on me." For whatever was

---

5. David Hansen, *The Art of Pastoring: Ministry without All the Answers* (Downers Grove, IL: InterVarsity Press, 1994), 38.

written in former days was written for our instruction, that through endurance and through the encouragement of the Scriptures we might have hope. May the God of endurance and encouragement grant you to live in such harmony with one another, in accord with Christ Jesus, that together you may with one voice glorify the God and Father of our Lord Jesus Christ. Therefore welcome one another as Christ has welcomed you, for the glory of God.

The Christians envisioned here are enjoying a harmony of doctrine, to be sure, but they are enjoying more than that. They are enjoying a harmony of what that doctrine, truly believed, produces. They are enjoying a harmonious culture. Ray Ortlund reminds us,

> Gospel doctrine creates a gospel culture. The doctrine of grace creates a culture of grace. When the doctrine is clear and the culture is beautiful, that church will be powerful. But there are no shortcuts to getting there. Without the doctrine, the culture will be weak. Without the culture, the doctrine will seem pointless.[6]

In a gospel culture, the doctrine is cherished all the more because we know it is the strength behind our bearing with each other's failings, our pleasing each other, our enduring with each other, and even our *outdoing one another* in showing honor (Rom. 12:10).

A church that wants this sweetness must center on the

---

6. Ray Ortlund, *The Gospel: How the Church Portrays the Beauty of Christ*, Building Healthy Churches (Wheaton, IL: Crossway, 2014), 21.

gospel, for the gospel is the only source of this sweetness. "May the God of endurance and encouragement grant you to live in such harmony" (Rom. 15:5). Paul knows this gospel culture can only come from God. And it will not come from the theoretical God of a gospel-centrality that amounts to little more than a church's wallpaper. It will come from the Spirit of God who brings conviction, comfort, and counsel through his Word, and who bids us in that Word to "welcome one another as Christ has welcomed you" (Rom. 15:7).

## A Repentant Spirit and a Hunger for Grace

Drift from gospel-centrality begins when an insensitivity to the presence of God begins. As such, Christians and Christian churches that want to avoid drifting away from a focus on grace will commit themselves to the humbling practice of prayer.

Understanding the connection between the gospel and prayer is very important. Initially, we understand that to receive the gospel (1 Cor. 15:1), we will likely pray a prayer of conversion. We acknowledge God's authority and his holiness. We confess our lostness to him. We profess our belief in his Son, Jesus, and in Jesus' work on the cross and out of the grave. We ask for forgiveness. We commit to Christ's lordship. The particular vocabulary may vary from prayer to prayer, but these are the typical elements of a prayer of conversion. It is after conversion that we sometimes struggle to connect prayer to the gospel.

Most Christians certainly view prayer as important to maintain a personal relationship with Jesus. We obviously view prayer as important for a life of blessing. But do we see how the act of prayer, similar to the practice of reading God's Word, puts us in a position of utter humility—of irreducible faith—in order to receive wholly from God?

We study God's Word because we cannot live on bread alone (Deut. 8:3). We need his Word to live. His Word is grace to sinners, and we pray because we are wholly reliant on God to live. "You do not have, because you do not ask" (James 4:2).

Committed prayer is commitment to the gospel because prayer represents the fundamental posture of the gospel—we are sinners with nothing but need. The grace we need to live is totally outside of ourselves. We do not have what it takes. Only the Lord can save us, just as only the Lord can supply all of our needs (Phil. 4:19).

Do you have the perception that evangelical churches are known for their extraordinary prayer? Are our prayer meetings as popular as our preaching conferences? Are our prayers during the worship gathering heartfelt, substantive, and sincere? Do they show presumption? Or do they show weakness, surrender?

I wonder if the real reason the gospel-centered movement seemed to sputter out is because we were a preaching, writing, and thinking tribe, but we weren't much of a praying tribe. No tribe that drifts into prayerlessness can expect to stay anchored to gospel-centrality for long.

It has been said that every major revival throughout

church history has been precipitated by strong biblical preaching. I am sure that is true. But I also believe that every major revival throughout church history has been precipitated by the desperate prayers of desperate people.

As we fill our religious appetites with all the offerings available to us in our church programs and through books, conferences, podcasts, social media, let us take great care that we do not become drunkenly neglectful of our soul's need for grace. The Spirit will bring revival according to his own timing, but I doubt he will bring it to an unrepentant people satisfied with themselves.

Gospel-centrality "works" in communities where people constantly turn to it as the only source of the grace we feel famished without.

A church that is intentionally in touch with its own emptiness apart from God's grace will also see the emptiness of self-interest and insular preoccupations. A truly gospel-centered church will not suffer much from "mission creep," the gradual drift from biblical objectives for the church due to distracting influences. The people will see the outside world not as enemies, assets or liabilities, inconveniences to our concerns, or impediments to our comfort, but as fellow image bearers, and thus as persons who are lost and in need of the very gospel we love.

Joe Thorn writes,

> When the gospel is central in a church, the church goes out into the world on mission while preserving its counter-cultural character as the people of God. The gospel-centered

church is driven by love—for God and others—which leads to joyful obedience that points back to God.[7]

As we sit around the table of our fellowship, enjoying the bread of life, we realize there's more than enough to go around. There's so much that we are more than satisfied, and we can't help but offer some to anybody who passes by the window.

Is no one passing by the window? Then by all means, let's go outside and start searching for people who will join us at the feast. There are always plenty of seats, and there is always plenty of gospel.

A repentant spirit and a hunger for grace make for "easy" preaching. What I mean is, as a climate of judgment recedes and a joyful expectation of grace increases, a congregation rejoices to hear the gospel preached. They do not measure every rhetorical technique or parse every word or pick every nit. They are Bereans, of course, holding their leaders accountable for faithful exposition of the inerrant Scriptures, but they are eager recipients of the gospel. The gospel is what they want. The gospel is what they're starving for. The gospel is what they go home feeling satisfied about. They're disappointed when you wander too far into speculative territory. They're discouraged by inordinate focus on political wrangling. They're offended by angry rants and bored by inspirational fluff. "Sir," they say, "we wish to see Jesus" (John 12:21).

And the reality is, the more we get in touch with our

---

7. Joe Thorn, *The Heart of the Church: The Gospel's History, Message, and Meaning* (Chicago: Moody, 2017), 12.

own need for Christ and our own hunger and thirst for his righteousness, the more adrift we will feel when we are adrift! To the spiritually hungry, only the gospel satisfies.

## The Gospel versus the Gospel-Centered Movement

Now we revisit a question from earlier in the book. What happened to the gospel-centered movement?

To be honest, I don't know. I suspect that as with all movements throughout church history, including good ones that last for a long time, there was a point at which the gospel-centered movement had run its course. Sometimes the Spirit appoints particular seasons of church culture for certain spiritual emphases in order to correct certain courses or do incisive work in specific areas. Sometimes these seasons produce century-spanning commitments across huge swaths of Christendom. Other times they pop up for only slivers of time and have different degrees of effects upon individual Christians and individual churches.

For all of that consideration, it is just true that Christian movements come and go. All such movements have an expiration date.

Whether the gospel-centered movement was worth it or not may then be left to individual appraisal. For some, it only gave us more celebrity Christianity, more abusive evangelicalism, more hypocrisy, more "liberal drift." For others, it gave us helpful vocabulary and good reminders of historic truths.

Should we even care?

I am not especially interested in convincing anyone to care—in a devotional way, at least—about the gospel-centered movement of the last couple of decades. But I do think it's worth caring about renewal movements in general. Even if you do not think this particular movement constituted any kind of renewal, it is helpful to think about what a true move of spiritual renewal would entail.

Tim Keller says renewal movements begin with extraordinary prayer, gospel application (by which he means the right understanding of the gospel and its implications for life and ministry), and gospel rediscovery.[8]

You may or may not resonate with that description, but I think it's fairly accurate.

I do think the gospel-centered movement produced renewal for many believers, and my only disappointment is that so many former adherents have since moved on. It makes me wonder if what they discovered in the movement was not the gospel per se but a new tribe to join. And when that tribe lost its appeal, its popularity, or maybe its own integrity, it proved itself worth graduating from. But if being in that tribe taught me anything about renewal movements, it's that latter part of Keller's definition: Renewal is empowered by gospel rediscovery.

We desperately need again today a rediscovery of the gospel.

I am astonished at how quickly we have deserted the centrality of grace. Not that there's anything else worth turning to! But we've done it anyway. And I pray the Lord will turn us

---

8. Timothy Keller, *Center Church: Doing Balanced, Gospel-Centered Ministry in Your City* (Grand Rapids: Zondervan, 2012), 73–74.

back again. Not to another series of conferences and programs, or another run of books or podcasts. Not even to a new set of tribal lingo. We can do without all that. I pray he will turn us back again to what we can't do without: the incomparable grace of the unadulterated gospel of Jesus Christ.

Maybe all of our drift of late, in all of these different directions, is going to send us over some waterfalls. Maybe the evangelical departures from gospel-centrality will quickly be interrupted by the messes we are making of our fellowships and the tarnishing we are doing to our witness. Maybe all of the distractions will prove personally ruinous for us as we are left with nothing to save us but the grace of God.

The first book to signal that a new gospel-centered *whatever* was afoot was probably Collin Hansen's *Young, Restless, Reformed*. It has aged . . . interestingly. At the conclusion of Hansen's final chapter, which is a provocative tour of the Mark Driscoll phenomenon, he recounts this line Driscoll said: "The guys who read Paul and want to fight for his doctrine should have an equal amount of zeal to follow in his example. . . . A lot of Calvinists talk like Paul; they don't act like him."[9]

I don't know all that has gone into Driscoll's processing and ultimate rejection of the movement that made him a celebrity, but I do know he was right the first time. I don't even know if he really believed it then, but it was true then, and it's true now. It is not enough to mimic Pauline rhetoric. We must embrace Paul's commitments.

9. Collin Hansen, *Young, Restless, Reformed: A Journalist's Journey with the New Calvinists* (Wheaton, IL: Crossway, 2008), 152.

Imitate me, as I also imitate Christ. (1 Cor. 11:1 CSB)

For I decided to know nothing among you except Jesus Christ and him crucified. (1 Cor. 2:2)

Is the gospel-centered movement dead?

I don't know. Maybe. But I know the gospel isn't.

Movements come and go. We can do without them. But gospel-centered churches we must not live without. Whether the gospel is in season or out of season, it will always be the order of the day.

Carl F. H. Henry once claimed, "The supernaturalist framework of historic Christianity is . . . the lone solution of modern dilemmas."[10]

Do you believe that?

I do. And I do not see how we will avoid the temptations of efficiency, security, and power and resist the currents of victimhood, spiritual dryness, superficiality, pragmatism, and the new legalism if we do not realign our Christian framework using the plumb line of Christ's powerful gospel.

Therefore we must pay much closer attention to what we have heard, lest we drift away from it. (Heb. 2:1)

---

10. Henry, *Uneasy Conscience*, 57.

# Conclusion

MATT CHANDLER TOLD A STORY ONCE ABOUT BEING backstage at a Christian leadership conference when a well-known fellow speaker said to him, "You must be 'the Bible guy.'" Chandler thought to himself, *Shouldn't we* all *be the Bible guy?*

I have had my own brushes with this appearance of novelty because of my commitments to gospel-centrality. While speaking at a men's conference in Florida almost a decade ago, the organizer explained to me, "We try to get a good variety of speakers for our guys to hear from. Expose them to different voices and influences." I nodded pleasantly. He added, "You're our first 'gospel guy.'"

I thought, *Shouldn't we* all *be gospel guys?*

Evidently, for many the answer is no. Many former "gospel guys" are now explicitly "law guys" while some are stealthily "law guys." Some are now culture war guys. Others are politics guys. Others have retreated back to being attractional guys or theological minutiae guys. There are as many types of guys as there are interests in the church and in the world.

I am praying that God will raise up a new generation of gospel guys. I'm praying he'll raise up so many, in fact, that being a gospel guy will not seem weird to anybody except unbelievers. Being a gospel guy will be normal!

But I realize that will pose a danger of its own. For when we assume the gospel, we are susceptible to losing it.

So perhaps the order of our day is to embrace the weirdness. To own the offense of the cross, even to the church. To stand upon the rock over which so many stumble and say, "Here I stand. I could do other, but I dare not!"

There's plenty of room. It doesn't look like much from afar, and standing here will put you at odds with a lot of people, including many evangelicals. They will call you names. Sad to say, but if you're loud enough and enjoy the gospel raucously enough, they may even write stuff about you on the internet.

But it will be worth it. When we get to the finish line, not a single one of us will regret we resolved to know nothing among each other but Christ and him crucified. He won't rebuke us for it. He won't say we wasted our time. It will all have been a preparation for the fixation we will enjoy for all eternity. If a resolute focus on the wonder of God's grace in Christ is good enough for the splendor of the infinite heaven, it's certainly good enough among the finite and fallen distractions of earth.

# Acknowledgments

THIS IS THE HARDEST BOOK I'VE EVER WRITTEN. Throughout its composition, I experienced countless awkward fits and starts, several elongated periods of melancholy, a few anxiety attacks, three illnesses, and the longest bouts of writer's block I've ever faced. I also gained back twenty of the forty pounds I'd lost before I started writing.

But now it's in your hands, so nobody can say I didn't get it done.

It took me much longer than I expected and much longer than I'd promised. Therefore, I am exceedingly grateful for the good people at Zondervan Publishers, especially editors Kyle Rohane and Ryan Pazdur. You've been much more patient than I deserve.

*Muchas gracias, tambien, a mi gente y agente*, Don Gates. Your unflagging enthusiasm keeps me keepin' on. I'll move on to that '80s music book now.

My employers and colleagues at Midwestern Baptist Theological Seminary and Spurgeon College, where I have the incredible honor of serving as Author in Residence, have been champions of my writing from the very beginning, and it's such a blessing to write among this cheerful community.

My fellow pastors and the congregation at Liberty Baptist Church remind me regularly that the gospel works and is worth it. Thank you for receiving the good news from every text, every single week without complaint and instead with great joy. Who is my boast? Is it not you?

Second to last, but not least, major praise to my wife, Becky, who I think was more nervous about running behind on this project than any other project I've undertaken before, but rolled with it graciously, encouraged me, made me coffee and brownies and nachos and a space to take breaks when my brain was mush. I love you to the moon and back.

Finally, and supremely, to the King eternal, immortal, invisible, the only wise God, be honor and glory for ever and ever. Amen. And, Jesus, thanks for the gifts.

# The Gospel-Driven Church

## Uniting Church Growth Dreams with the Metrics of Grace

*Jared C. Wilson*

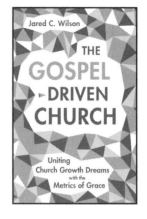

Many evangelical churches face the problem of the open "back door"—even as new people arrive, older members are leaving, looking for something else. Combined with this problem is the discipleship deficit, the difficult truth that most evangelicals are not reaching the unchurched at the rates they think they are. In fact, many of the metrics that we often "count" in the church to highlight success really don't tell us the full story of a church's spiritual state. Things like attendance, decisions, dollars, and experiences can tell us something about a church, but not everything.

To cultivate a spiritually healthy church we need a shift in our metrics—a "grace-shift" that prioritizes the work of God in the lives of people over numbers and dollars, asking questions like:

Are people growing in their esteem for Jesus?

Is there a dogged devotion to the Bible as the ultimate authority for life?

Is there a growing interest in theology and doctrine?

Does the congregation show a discernible spirit of repentance?

Does the church have evident love for God and for our neighbors in the congregation?

Leading a church culture to shift from numerical success to the metrics of grace can be costly, but leaders who have conviction, courage, and commitment can lead while avoiding some of the landmines that often destroy churches. Wilson includes diagnostic questions that will help leaders measure—and lead team transparency in measuring as a group—the relative spiritual health of their church, as well as a practical prescriptive plan for implementing this metric-measuring strategy without becoming legalistic.

# Gospel-Driven Ministry

## An Introduction to the Calling and Work of a Pastor

*Jared C. Wilson*

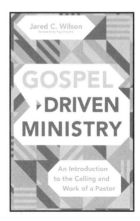

From the beginning of his ministry, Jesus called and equipped individuals who would serve his community of followers. These "shepherds" are called to preach, pray, and care for the needs of God's people. But what does it mean to be a pastor? And what is the nature of this ministry, according to the Bible?

In *Gospel-Driven Ministry*, Jared Wilson begins by looking at the qualifications for the pastorate, addressing the notion of a call to ministry and how an individual—and a church community—can best identify the marks of maturity and affirm a call. In each chapter, Wilson looks at one of the core practices of pastoral ministry, including:

Preaching Sermons
Developing a Vibrant Prayer Life
Caring and Counseling
Pastoring Married and Single
Gospel-Centered Leadership
Fighting Sin and Spiritual Warfare
Resolving Conflict
Passing on the Ministry to Others

In addition, Wilson provides practical resources including theological insights on baptism and the Lord's Supper, guidance for wedding and funeral sermons, outlines for leading elder and deacon meetings, tips for interviewing new pastors, questions to ask at ordination, and advice on knowing when and how to leave a pastor role. This is a comprehensive, practical guide to pastoral ministry that prepares new pastors and equips those currently serving for long-term, healthy ministry.

# The Storied Life

## Christian Writing as
## Art and Worship

*Jared C. Wilson*

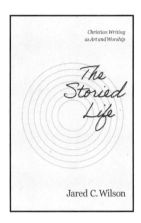

In *The Storied Life*, veteran author Jared C. Wilson explores the ins and outs of writers and writing, exploring the myriad ways the craft is more about transformation than simply communication. From decades of experience and with his signature wit, Wilson brings well-earned insight, autobiographical reflections, and meaningful meditations to the topic of writing as a way of life and as a way of worship, showing how the concept of Story—our personal stories and God's grand story of redemption—shapes fiction and nonfiction writers alike.

Chapters focus on topics like:
The liturgy of story.
Writing as a spiritual act.
Perseverance and endurance.
Writing as a calling.
Promotion, publishing, and platform.

Whether you're a long-time writer or a beginning author, a daily journaler or an occasional dabbler, *The Storied Life* will help you improve your craft. It will lead you to think more deeply about the disciplines and dispositions needed to write for transformation.